Indian Business Case Studies

Indian Business Case Studies

Volume VIII

SRILATHA PALEKAR

ARUN PARDHI

SUNANDA JINDAL

Indian Case Studies in Business Management

OXFORD
UNIVERSITY PRESS

Great Clarendon Street, Oxford, ox2 6dp,
United Kingdom

Oxford University Press is a department of the University of Oxford.
It furthers the University's objective of excellence in research, scholarship,
and education by publishing worldwide. Oxford is a registered trade mark of
Oxford University Press in the UK and in certain other countries

© ASM Group of Institutes, Pune, India 2022

The moral rights of the authors have been asserted

First Edition published in 2022

Published in the United States of America by Oxford University Press
198 Madison Avenue, New York, NY 10016, United States of America

British Library Cataloguing in Publication Data

Data available

Library of Congress Control Number: 2022938091

ISBN 978-0-19-286944-9

DOI: 10.1093/oso/9780192869449.001.0001

Dr R.R. Pachpande
[1947–2009]

'Education is the Soul of our society'

The series editors and the volume authors of the Case Volumes titled as 'Indian Business Case Studies', published by Oxford University Press, have a deep sense of gratefulness while dedicating these Case Volumes to the memory of Dr Raghunath R. Pachpande, the founder of ASM Group of Institutes, Pune, India

It was with the untiring efforts and Strategic Vision of Dr R.R. (as he was known to his close friends and colleagues) which has been instrumental in ASM Group adopting case methodology as a unique element in its pedagogy which motivated the faculty and students of ASM Group of Institutes to develop business case studies on Indian businesses and use them to teach management subjects in all branches of business management studies.

Dr R.R. Pachpande was a leader beyond parlance and ahead of time in establishing educational institutes, more so in higher studies in business management, specifically in the industrial belts in the state of Maharashtra with a view to providing the best of experiential learning to its students through closer interactions with business units around.

Today, ASM Group continues the great legacy of Dr R.R. Pachpande under the leadership of his successors and who have succeeded in taking ASM Group to global recognition as a unique group of institutes offering world-class education in all branches of business management.

This Case Volume is dedicated to the memories of the late Dr R.R. Pachpande.

Contents

SECTION II CASE STUDIES IN
FINANCE MANAGEMENT

SECTION III MULTIDISCIPLINARY CASE STUDIES

Preface

Many universities and management institutes across the globe have adopted the case study methodology for teaching almost all branches of management studies for several decades. This trend has been seen in India also, wherein the Indian Institutes of Management (IIMs) and progressive management institutes in the private sector have implemented case methodology as an important pedagogical tool in business management education.

However, there is a severe shortage in Indian business case studies faced by the B-schools in India and those global institutes associated with Indian academia. The majority of the case studies studied at IIMs and other A-grade B-schools in India are from situations in industries in foreign countries and have very little or no relevance to Indian business situations. This acts as a major gap for faculty and student engagement in business management studies both at UG and masters level (PG) studies, where clarification of theoretical concepts is possible mainly through f use of case methodology, which enables insight into business real-life business situations.

Besides, the objectives and purposes for which case studies are developed abroad are much different from the course of studies in Indian B-schools. Therefore, the dependence on foreign case studies for Indian students does not provide any real situational insight into Indian business. Although the curriculum requires taking the students through case study methodology, there are not many Indian case studies for this purpose.

Major objectives of use of case study methodology (use of business cases)

The main objectives of using case-based teaching as a major pedagogical tool in B-schools are as follows:

1. To facilitate students' concept development capabilities through exposure to real-life problems in Industries
2. To enable students to correlate theoretical topics with the techniques used in analysing complex issues in business situations

3. To develop skills using which students can develop application matrix for the theoretical topics for real-life problem analysis and resolution techniques

4. Help the students of B-schools to develop orientation towards the important attributes and attitudinal requirements for effective handling of complex situations at the workplace

5. To develop a clear understanding of the techniques used for problem analysis, situation analysis and decision analysis and appropriate understanding of the difference between problems and situations in management

6. To develop the group-based approaches to solving problems and challenges at the workplace by appropriate coordination of and collaboration with all related aspects of a situation

7. To develop a reference manual for recording the problems tackled and the essential lessons learnt from past incidences for use in future eventualities of recurrence of issues

8. To develop the preventive steps that must be initiated to ensure the problems resolved once do not recur in the immediate future

Business case studies are basically oriented towards developing the evaluative and analytical skills of students towards industry situations. Such case studies draw the attention of participants of the case resolution methodology on the in-depth correlative evaluation of the issues in the case study with the various related topics that the students have to study about in their classrooms. These case studies could be on issues related to human resources, industrial relations, product and process, marketing, and finance management areas in business management.

The academic environment across the world, too, is facing a major disruption on account of the global pandemic COVID 19, forcing the offline education system to switch over to online/blended versions of the teaching and learning process. And the use of case methodology and simulation exercises are the main in gradients for sustaining effective ways of delivering experiential learning through the use of case and case lets in an online mode of teaching, ensuring student engagements and online interactive ways of knowledge dissemination.

Oxford University Press, in association with ASM Group of Institutes Pune, India, is publishing for the first time a comprehensive Case Volumes as series of eight volumes with case studies on Indian Businesses selected from all aspects of business functions like HR, finance marketing, and operations, and providing an exciting and long waited opportunity to faculty and students across the globe to access Indian business case studies through these Case Volumes.

We are very confident that the Case Volumes will receive a very good response and will be of utmost use to the readers.

Acknowledgements

The series editors wish to acknowledge with thanks the contribution of data for the case studies from ASM's Academic Associates, the CETYS University Mexico—Dr Scott Venezia, Dean International Affairs and Dr Francisco Velez Dean of Colleges, and Dr Paulina Garcia CETYS Mexico.

As also of several senior faculty from ASM Group of Institutes for their help in proofreading and editing the case studies.

We also acknowledge the numerous news reporters of daily news-papers in business and economics in India, which have been rich and authentic secondary data sources for the design and development of case studies for the Case Volumes.

About the Series Editors

Dr Sandeep Pachpande, Chairman,
ASM Group of Institutes, Pune, India

Prof J. A. Kulkarni, Professor,
ASM Group of Institutes, Pune, India

Both the series editors have decades of experience in business case design and development and also implementation of case methodology of teaching for the faculty and students of business schools in India and abroad.

The series editors have to their credit for authoring three major books on business case studies published by globally known publishers and in conducting workshops for case design and development.

The series editors have a very good network with leaders and stalwarts in business management studies across the globe and are popular as keynote speakers in many national and international conferences. They have a very rich experience in organizing national and international conferences and case competitions.

Currently, the series editors are busy completing a unique case analysis and resolution methodology program which is under copyright considerations.

Dr Sandeep Pachpande

Prof J.A. Kulkarni

About the Volume Authors

Dr Arun Pardhi
Bsc, LLB, MBA, Phd

Dr Arun Pardhi is currently engaged as professor in Human Resources Department at the ASM Group of Institutes Pune India

Experience
Industry
Dr Arun Pardhi has nearly 3 decades of rich experience in major manu-facturing Industries in India and is thoroughly exposed to management of ground level HR and IR. Dr Arun Pardhi has his credit introducing newer ER and Talent Management practices in Industries and has helped many budding executives to train and grow in their professions.

Academic
Dr Arun Pardhi has been a guest faculty for business management studies in Human Resources and has to his credit several national and interna-tional level research paper presentations

Publications
Dr Arun Pardhi has authored the following text and Reference Books for Management Studies

1. Human Resource Management (Success Publications Pvt Ltd India)

2. Research Methods and Techniques (Success Publications Pvt Ltd India)
3. Compensation Management & Derivatives (Success Publications Pvt Ltd India)

Dr Sunanda Jindal Bsc, MBA, PhD

Dr Sunanda Jindal is currently engaged as Professor at ASM Group of Institutes Pune India

Academic experience
Dr Sunanda Jindal has around 15 years of Academic Experience as professor for the MBA students in marketing specialization. As professor she has conducted several workshops and Case study competitions for inter collegiate events as also in mock marketing exercises for the students as to improve ground level exposure of the students in marketing dynamics.

Publications
Dr Sunanda has presented more than 15 research papers in national and international conferences published in top ranked journals, including UGC CARE. Dr Sunanda has worked as editor for the review of research papers for Emerald Journals and other journals of International repute.

Dr Srilatha Tushar Palekar
MCom, MBA, PhD (Marketing)

Dr Srilatha Palekar is currently engaged at ASM Group of Institutes Pune India as professor for the MBA students specializing in Marketing Management

Academic Experience
Dr Srilatha has 15 years of academic experience in teaching and coaching students and industry executives in areas of marketing management

Publications
Dr Srilatha has to her credit more than 15 research papers presented at national Conferences as also few in Research Journals.

Awards
Dr Srilatha has been conferred with a coveted award from the Government of India for the contribution on welfare and upliftment of the women from weaker section in the society.

Business Case Studies—Relevance to Management Education

Many B-schools outside India have adopted decades ago the case study methodology for teaching almost all branches of management studies. This trend has been seen in India also, wherein a majority of the Indian Institutes of Management (IIMs) have implemented case study-based methodology as an important pedagogical tool in business management education. The major issue in India is, however, the inadequate interaction between B-schools and industries. The fault lies with both B-schools and the industry. The B-schools, in a majority of cases, cannot provide research-based solutions to industry problems due to a lack of necessary infrastructure and facilities. And the industries, in the absence of any direct benefit from the institutes, are not inclined to waste their time and funds on B-school education.

Hence, there is a severe shortage in Indian case studies through which the B-schools can provide industry insight to their students. The majority of the case studies studied at IIMs and other A-grade B-schools are imported from abroad. These case studies are from situations in industries in foreign countries and have very little or no relevance to Indian students who have to necessarily study the situations in Indian industries. It is also true that foreign universities wanting to educate and train students interested in understanding Indian business practices also do not have case studies on Indian businesses to use in their case methodology of teaching.

It is today a matter of the fact that business schools like Harvard and Stanford follow case methodology for 80 per cent of the graduate and post-graduate studies for business management courses. The world around the trend involves students 70 per cent studying through experiential learning methods like case studies and spend just around 20% in faculty-led classroom lecture sessions

Besides, the objectives and purposes for which case studies are developed abroad are much different from the level and course of studies in

Indian B-schools. Therefore, the dependence on foreign case studies for Indian students does not provide any real situational insight into Indian business. Although the syllabus for management studies requires taking the students through case study methodology, unfortunately, there are not many Indian case studies that can be discussed with the students.

Thus, it is a Catch-22 situation. Unless institutes have the capability and the required infrastructure to cater to industry-related issues, they cannot expect any interactive support from the industries; unless institutes get adequate data from industries, their teaching content and quality continue to be much less than the expectations of the industry from students who pass out from such institutes.

Objectives of Use of Case Study Methodology

The main objectives of using case-based teaching as a major pedagogical tool in B-schools are as follows:

1. To facilitate students' concept development capabilities through exposure to real-life problems in industries
2. To enable students to correlate theoretical topics with the techniques used in analysing complex issues in business situations
3. To develop skills using which students can develop application matrix for the theoretical topics for real-life problem analysis and resolution techniques
4. Help the students of B-schools to develop orientation towards the important attributes and attitudinal requirements for effective handling of complex situations at the workplace
5. To develop a clear understanding of the techniques used for problem analysis, situation analysis, and decision analysis and appropriate understanding of the difference between problems and situations in management
6. To develop the group-based approaches to solving problems and challenges at the workplace by appropriate coordination of and collaboration with all related aspects of a situation

7. To develop a reference manual for recording the problems tackled and the essential lessons learnt from past incidences for use in future eventualities of recurrence of issues
8. To develop the preventive steps that must be initiated to ensure the problems resolved once do not recur in the immediate future

Types of Case Studies

The entire gamut of business case studies can be classified as follows:

1. Evaluative case studies (teaching case studies)
2. Task- or action-oriented case studies (including project-based case studies)
3. Research-oriented case studies—case research

Application of Case Methodology in Business Management Studies

Teaching case studies are basically oriented towards developing the evaluative and analytical skills of students towards industry situations. Such case studies draw the attention of participants of the case resolution methodology on the in-depth correlative evaluation of the issues in the case study with the various related topics that the students have to study about in their classrooms. These case studies could be on issues related to human resources, industrial relations, product and process, marketing, and finance management areas in business management.

Such case studies help the students mainly to examine their understanding of evaluative steps such as evaluation of the financial situation of a company or the quality aspects of its products and services, etc. The task- or action-oriented case studies dwell on business issues that call for appropriate decision-making capabilities of executives. By involving students of management studies in the resolution activity of such case studies, the skills learnt by them through the theoretical studies can be experimented in the resolution exercises.

The students can be motivated to apply their decision-making skills along with their risk management ability to make business decisions. Developing a plan of actions oriented towards the resolution of the case issues calls for effective role-play techniques as also presentation skills from the part of students; they are normally required to defend their plan of approach and decisions in front of other students and the faculty, which helps them improve their capabilities to sustain questions and criticisms, normal features in business management.

Research-based case studies, as the name suggests, involve students in research initiatives to establish a hypothesis or to disprove a common belief, which influence the progress and sustenance of business ideologies or even scientific or technical aspects of business dynamics. These case studies normally call for prerequisites such as thorough business knowledge and enough exposure to both the theoretical and practical aspects of the issues presented in the case studies. Issues of corporate governance and social welfare functions, which have both obligatory and voluntary elements attached to them, are pursued in research studies to establish the utility purposes of such aspects, which range from free will to a compelled activity.

However, the real problem today for B-schools is the non-availability of good case studies on Indian business. Recently, it was reported that IIMs (IIM Bangalore) are resorting to appointing consultants to develop case studies on Indian enterprises, since the usage of imported case studies from foreign businesses is fast losing its relevance to the Indian business scenario, which in itself has unique features among the global economies. India, which is rated as the world's fourth-largest economy, definitely needs specific and separate approaches to the case study methodology as a pedagogical tool for B-school studies.

The Present Environment

The academic environment across the world is facing a major disruption on account of the global pandemic COVID 19, forcing the offline education to switch over to online/blended versions of teaching and learning process. And the use of case methodology and simulation exercises are the main in gradients while maintaining the effective ways of delivering experiential learning through the use of case and case lets in an online mode of teaching, ensuring student engagements and online interactive ways of knowledge dissemination. Realizing this requirement, even globally reputed institutes such as Harvard and MIT Sloan have made case method of teaching as essential parts of their online courses.

ASM Group, with nearly 250 business case studies developed by its faculty over the years, takes pleasure in offering these cases mostly on Indian businesses through these Case Volumes to the faculty, students as also for executive education programs. The case studies are selected from ASM's Captive Case Bank as most appropriate for the current day syllabi and on Indian business scenarios, including select live case studies on ongoing businesses.

ASM Group is certain that the Case Volumes as published will receive excellent response from the faculty and students alike in B-schools in India and abroad.

SECTION I
CASE STUDIES IN HUMAN RESOURCES

HR, Entrepreneurship, CSR, CG, and Sustainability

1. A Botched-Up Succession Plan
2 Entrepreneurial Excellence
3. Corporate Governance under Threat?
4. Transformational Leadership
5. Dishends Pvt Ltd
6. The Tiny Owl
7. Bosch is the Boss
8. Enterprise and Ethics
9. Corporate Social Responsibility

1

A Botched-Up Succession Plan

A Case Study on Succession Issues at Tata

Learning Objectives

All across the globe, the issue of succession planning in family-managed organizations and organizations having its promoter and founding directors has been one of the difficult exercises in ensuring continuity of visionary, missionary zeal and overall business ethos and ethics as aligned to time-tested and normated core values and business approaches.

The issue of succession planning in such companies is fraught with dominance of traditionalism over casualty and indifferent not so serious outlook towards core values.

Indian large companies like the Tata Group, Infosys, Birla are no exception to this in spite of enormous scrutiny and observation and evaluation over time and by expert teams for the selection of a suitable successor to the incumbent leader the succession has led to unprecedented board room battles at times leading to unceremonious exit of the successor CEO.

It is therefore necessary for the students of management studies to study and analyse such incidences with long-term solutions, especially when the effects of generation gaps on existing core values and ways of doing business. This case narrates the succession debacle at Tata Group, which took nearly five years for board room disturbance to settle down.

Synopsis

When transfer of managerial authority is not accompanied by ownership change, the predecessor continues to call the shots. In all the excitement generated by the recent events in the Tata group, where the chairman was

Indian Business Case Studies. Srilatha Palekar, Arun Pardhi and Sunanda Jindal, Oxford University Press. © ASM Group of Institutes, Pune, India 2022. DOI: 10.1093/oso/9780192869449.003.0001

replaced by his predecessor—albeit as an interim measure—the real issue has gone into hiding.

A substantial focus of the discussions and comments from the press, observers, and experts has been on procedures and personalities. Whether the incumbent chairman was given adequate notice about his removal and whether he was given a chance to argue his case is no doubt relevant questions to assess the fairness of the decision. But these questions speak to the procedural issues surrounding corporate governance. The other widely discussed question is about the differing perspectives and the positions taken by the incumbent and the predecessor. But if one were to seriously search for the root cause of this issue, it is possible to recognize the elephant in the room—ineffective succession planning and implementation.

Succession planning is one issue that not many business organizations have handled well. While it can be quite challenging and tricky in family-owned and managed companies, we also have examples of other companies promoted by professionals struggling in this area. What comes in the way of highly reputed and sensible business leaders delivering on this inevitable but crucial mandate given to them in their role as business leaders and owners?

Ownership Transfer

Let us take the case when the incumbent leader represents ownership interests and also functions as the executive head. When this leader has to put in place a successor, and plans for it, organizational succession always assumes prominence, and ownership succession recedes into the background. This kind of incomplete succession planning has serious implications for the effectiveness of the succession process as a whole. As a principal owner, the predecessor not only has the freedom to choose the timing of the succession event, but also a say in who the successor would be.

Once a successor is in place, the predecessor relinquishes the management role, but still gets to play the ownership role—either from close quarters as a member of the board or from a distance as the principal shareholder acting through other informal forums or through nominees.

In effect, they continue to be in a position to pass judgment on the actions of the successor in one form or other.

Such an arrangement often makes life difficult for both the predecessor and the successor. Being continually exposed to the ongoing affairs of the organization which he or she no longer has the mandate to lead, the predecessor is emotionally challenged to distinguish between decisions that are a response to changing business environment, and those that imply a possible dilution of legacy—of the group or family or the individual. Or, the moves may be seen as a neglect of the legitimate interests of the principal shareholders.

The successor also finds himself or herself in a predicament of having to put his or her decisions through multiple screens, some of which might amount to just blind guesses about whether the decision will be acceptable. Given that innumerable decisions get taken in multi-business conglomerates almost on a daily business, this field of discomfort only expands forever and without anyone being able to predict when it will explode.

Clean Break

What can be done then? There are very simple solutions but they have to be implemented with maturity and iron will. First, it is well accepted amongst family business scholars that succession means the predecessor gives up control and the successor assumes responsibility. This spirit behind succession needs to be understood by all the family business leaders who make way for a successor. When the predecessors give up control, they should not only give up control over the management, but also give up control over the ownership interest. They should find a successor to play the owners' role, irrespective of whether a legal transfer of ownership happens or not.

Once a successor is put in place, the predecessor should also steadfastly sever all connections with the business. This is possible only under one condition—that the predecessor takes up other pursuits in life. Most predecessors refuse to cut the umbilical cord with business under the guise of ensuring continuity. It is not without reason that succession is also metaphorically compared to passing the baton. In a relay race, the continuity is provided by running along with the successor before passing the baton, but not after.

Sure, the predecessor can provide advice or opinion when specifically asked by the successor. But he or she should refrain from any involvement that goes beyond providing that advice. Such advice should also be provided with no expectations that it will be accepted or implemented, either partly or fully. Generally, a predecessor is fully involved in the process of selecting a successor. That being the case, the predecessor should own up his or her choice of the successor and fully accept the consequences—even if those include erosion of business value and personal or family wealth. Keeping the back door open to second guess successor's actions and to pull the rug from under the successor's feet only means that the succession has not happened in spirit.

Governance Mechanisms

On the other hand, if organizational succession is implemented along with ownership succession, the new representatives of ownership interests will play their role, without carrying the emotional burdens of the predecessor, of holding the successor accountable to good performance. They can do so through other governance mechanisms like the board and family council, which can be structured to function without the involvement of the predecessor. Some family business leaders in India consciously follow these principles, but it would be great if many follow suit. Only then will succession cease to be the Achilles' heel of Indian family business. The details are as narrated below.

Tata group was founded in 1868 by Jamsetji Tata. Today, it is a global enterprise, headquartered in India, comprising over 100 independent operating companies. The group operates in more than 100 countries across six continents, with a mission 'To improve the quality of life of the communities we serve globally, through long-term stakeholder value creation based on Leadership with Trust'. The board of Tata Sons stunned corporate India by firing Cyrus Mistry, who was steering the ship of Tata for the last four years as chairman, to bring into the job to Ratan Tata, who emerged from retirement to wrest back control of the group that bears his family name. Ratan Tata, who helmed the group for 21 years after being chosen as successor by his uncle JRD Tata, is credited with transforming the group through bold decisions, including large global acquisitions, even as some of his peers struggled to stay relevant after the economic liberalization of the early 1990s. During Tata's tenure, the group's revenue shot up to around Rs.4.76 trillion in 2011–2012 from Rs.10,000 crores in 1991. Tata made some notable acquisitions, starting from Tetley by Tata Tea for $450 million in 2000 to steelmaker Corus by Tata Steel in 2007 for £6.2 billion and the landmark Jaguar Land Rover in 2008 for $2.3 billion by Tata Motors. Cyrus Mistry was chosen by a five-member panel in 2012 to succeed Ratan Tata.

The Major Factors Leading to His Selection

Career achievements and financial knowledge.

Having majority of Tata Sons shares.

Experience of being an M.D in Shapoorji Pallonji Mistry's Construction Group.

Familiarity with the family of Tatas.

Young business leader with a modern outlook.

Hope to bring turnaround of the group.

Having certain character traits like his predecessor Ratan Tata namely, soft-spoken, candid, and down to earth.

Some of His Highlights as the Chairman in His Four Years Tenure

Financial disfigurement taken in Tata Steel, Tata Chemicals, and Indian Hotels as Mistry chased profits and not assets.

Urea business of Tata Chemicals sold to Norway-based Yara International's Indian unit for Rs 2,670 crores.

Pulled out application for license to set up commercial bank.

Market cap of top 10 listed firms up at Rs 8.21 lakh crores from Rs 4.66 lakh crores

Operating cash flows at the Tata group have soared over 30 per cent CAGR in the last three years.

Tata group has expanded into the defence manufacturing business.
Tata group's gross debt jumped by 2 per cent, but net debt decreased by
3.3 per cent; however, cash and equivalent assets grew by some 10
per cent. With some 70 per cent of Tata group revenue coming from
its international operations.
Mistry ensured the lion's share of capital expenditure went in that direction too and thereby virtually guaranteed no problems beset the
group's functioning there. The tenure of Cyrus Mistry has been a
mixed basket of achievements and failures.

Case Questions

1. It is really intriguing as to what was really expected of Mr Mistry
   as he started and allowed to perform for not less than four years,
   a fairly long period for continuity that too when the person appointed is from the Inner circle of the selection committee. Do you
   feel that there are more reasons for the sudden marching order than
   what is put out in the news? (Your comments and criticisms should
   respect the current norms of corporate culture and with due diligence to the reputation of individuals involved.)

2. A similar situation has arisen in an IT giant Infosys with an almost equal global footprint wherein also the executive prudence of
   the new CEO is being questioned by one of the founders. Do you
   think it is a generation gap or the feeling of drifting away from traditional much accepted and praised practices of erstwhile founders and trustees? What do you think would be the impact of such
   skirmishes on the employees and customers who look forward to
   sustainable business?

3. Do you also think a change as vividly asked for or picking up on
   strategic gaps in performance would ensure smooth compliance
   and corrections in apprehensions of drift in corporate governance
   as alleged.

2

Entrepreneurial Excellence

A Live Case Study on a Progressive Medium-Sized Enterprise

Learning Objectives

It is observed that for higher studies in business management, there is a dearth of real-life examples in terms of live or field researched case studies wherein the faculty and students can have access to the real-life entrepreneur to discuss and understand from the horse's mouth the various issues and characteristics of starting and growing the enterprise amidst a present-day situation of complexity and vagueness in sustainable business ventures. This case study offers a real-life journey of two young and promising entrepreneurs without the blessings of any inherited business empire. The innate desires and dreams to establish an enterprise merely as a challenge and lifetime opportunity is the real motivator for entrepreneurs to conquer all obstacles in both the external and internal environments and build courage, confidence, and credentials to succeed in realizing their dreams. Rather than bookish knowledge and classical definitions on entrepreneurship, it is better to understand that seeing and believing is definitely a better way for students who aspire to become successful entrepreneurs. Learning from a story is 'Ideology'; learning and believing after seeing is 'Reality'. The authors feel that the best way to teach and learn the basics of entrepreneurship is better served through real-life field researched case studies from current business environments. It is possible to either visit the unit or invite the entrepreneurs to the classroom sessions to share their real-life

Indian Business Case Studies. Srilatha Palekar, Arun Pardhi and Sunanda Jindal, Oxford University Press. © ASM Group of Institutes, Pune, India 2022. DOI: 10.1093/oso/9780192869449.003.0002

experiences in dealing with all challenges successfully in establishing their enterprise, including priority Dos and Don'ts ensuring entrepreneurial sustainability. Indian government is urging entrepreneurs to help the national economy by exploiting domestic and global opportunities under the Make in India call.

This case study is a right example wherein the entrepreneurs are striving hard to acquire capabilities to develop and supply high technology products and services in many fields, including import substitution.

Synopsis

In independent India, the birth, growth, and perpetuations of great entrepreneurial ventures in the small and medium segments have always been due to circumstances that in the fields of technology products to follow the foreign manufacturers and serve them with support activities for manufacture and services of less technical/mundane products such as sheet metal guards, washers, gaskets, castings, simple forgings, machining facilities, and similar requirements.

Entrepreneurs of rare calibre, such as Tatas, Walchands, Birlas, Bajaj, Mahindras, to name a few, even though they started with simpler products and services as accessories to foreign products, have only in the previous few decades come to be recognized as globally competitive producers of high technology products and services. If one sees the trend again, the concentration of rich otherwise, and traditionally business families, alone have been able to sustain and grow to be in the limelight.

However, the entrepreneurial spirit in genetically independent thinking and wanting to 'Wish to Do it' not 'Do as told' people not so lucky in business inheritance have in the majority of the cases been toiling as craftsmen or joined national services like the armed forces to satisfy their urge to prove themselves or settled in work in jobs giving some scope to their entrepreneurial urge in other's units.

But it is a matter of pride that few such soldiers on their relinquishing army jobs, on resettlement have enthused, coerced, cajoled their next-generation youth into seeking independence from employee status and choosing careers to be the courageous employers who support and protect others families and also serve the nation as well.

This case study is about one such family in the unbelievably rural, financially not so strong of Mr Lokhande and Mr Shinde's from a backward location in Satara in Maharashtra. Sr Mr Lokhande and Mr Shinde did not know each other before they both joined the Indian Army in the early 60s but during their service in the army, looking at the plight of dependence on imported equipment and spares etc., made a firm commitment to themselves that they will ensure the next generation from their respective families would undertake entrepreneurial ventures to manufacture in India the equipment and parts on which Indian government was highly dependent on foreign supplies.

With the above determination, Mr Lokhande and Mr Shinde from the next generation from the two families completed their respective studies in engineering from Satara doing daily travel up and down from their nearby villages with a single-minded focus on doing something special on their own after studies.

Today if one visits the two plants of Proto D Engineering (PDE) proudly owned and managed by Pradip and Dipak in MIDC Bhosari and Chakan in Pune, it is not surprising that one would be stuck by the 'Awe' to see the entrepreneurial excellence as a result of dedication and single-minded conviction and commitment and the perpetuating hunger of these young entrepreneurs have expressed to serve the country through product and process import substitution and growth plans fully attuned to the call of the nation the Make in India.

PDE is a standing example of what a singularly focused, strategically managed enterprise can achieve in a span of less than a decade. They are the unique suppliers of complex prototype components to all the major manufacturers of automobiles and other transport equipment manufacturers. The revenues catapulted from a meagre Rs 1 million in 2008 to a staggering Rs 700 million in a span of ten years (2016–2017) which has 100% import substitution content in its supplies, including tool designs and prototype components.

Proto D Engineering

A symbol of a successful entrepreneurial spirit in a challenging business scenario.

Case Details

Mr Lokhande and Mr Shinde, under guidance and advice from their respective fathers (ex-defence personnel) soon after their matriculation in the village, moved over to the nearby town of Satara in the early 90s to join Diploma Course in Engineering. Meticulously Mr Lokhande selected the production engineering and Mr Shinde selected electronics specialization, which very well supplemented/complimented each other. The common advice given to these youngsters was to:

1. Prepare to be successful entrepreneurs rather than look for jobs.
2. To do everything possible to manufacture products and services which substitute imports.
3. To prove that people from the home state of Maharashtra can succeed as entrepreneurs otherwise branded as mere job seekers.

Both Mr Lokhande and Mr Shinde were very well aware of the fact that both needed rigorous experience at the Shop floor levels of high precision engineering companies before they could define their entrepreneurial business idea. Hence, immediately after completing their studies as diploma engineers, they moved over to Pune by 1994 and worked with companies engaged in the tool room and tool engineering segments; they worked with M/S Profilo Form and Alfa Engineering Co. in MIDC Bhosari in tool design and tool manufacturing areas. For almost seven to eight years, both had forgotten all the life comforts, working continuously 24 × 7 at times for months without breaks, including neglect of regular meals and rest.

After initial experience and gaining certain confidence in managing high precision designs and tool manufacture, they now thought giving a try to their entrepreneurial urge of getting on their own, but they did not have the financial grip on investments required even though they were known as reliable technicians in the industries around by then.

In the year 2000–2001, both Mr. Shinde and Mr. Lokhande went on a week's hibernation to plan their strategies for their next moves. They did not have any jobs for a few days; even the family members were worried about what they were up to. According to the duo, this break was necessary experience on interactive thoughts on how and in which direction to steer their entrepreneurial purpose. They did visit a few of the customers of earlier employers and bankers met the MIDC officers and other government agencies and a few fellow entrepreneurs and likely investors, but the overall outcome was not very assuring and encouraging.

There was this small enterprise MPlus Co. which was mostly managed by the college friends of Mr Shinde and Mr Lokhande, seven to eight of them who had invested their personal funds to install a few second-hand machines and a borrowed industrial shed on rent and carrying out job work for other small units in CNC and similar facilities. It was here that they gathered some courage and decided to join MPlus as job agents to get job work from their earlier customers of Profilo Form and Alfa as also establish new customers for MPlus. In a way, their jobs were not as regular employees but commission agents on the revenue of jobs they get for MPlus; even the proprietors and promoters knew that both Mr Shinde and Mr Lokhande are free to fall out at any time or continue to take help later as and when required.

Birth of an Enterprise

Ultimately it was in 2008 that the entrepreneurial thought process of the duos could no longer wait and what resulted was a set up under the title 'Proto D Engineering' with Mr Lokhande and Mr Shinde as proprietors/partners in a rented shed in MIDC Bhosari not very far off from MPlus.

The initial investment was around Rs10 lakhs for the basic infrastructural and operational facilities. The sublime efforts of the duo during 2001–2007 to select the appropriate line of manufacture and the available financial assistance from various agencies, the certainty of available work from earlier contacts, including MPlus, had yielded enough clarity about the sustainable levels in the initial one to two years of Initial operations as an independent venture. The other family members were also kept in the loop for the best and the worst-case scenarios.

The Business Idea

After an exhaustive survey and understanding of absolute and growing requirements from major automobile companies in and around MIDC Pune and Chakan areas and the nature of shortfalls in delivery commitments, PDE, as the name suggests, decided to dig deep into 'Providing all essential and necessary design and development and manufacture of PROTO types for all the R&D (ERC) and Project departments of OE Customers such as Tata Motors, M&M ,Volkswagen, and many more.

Initial Financial Outlay

PDE had finalized to buy a few second-hand imported laser cutting machines and a few CNC machining centres, 3D measuring instruments, and other conventional machines, including material handling metal cutting sheers, press breaks, and many more special purpose equipment.

The funds required for the startup were to the tune of Rs 25–30 lakhs in a span of three to four years, which was arranged through hypothecation of machinery for long-term loans from Sholapur Bank (which was also the banker for MPlus). The overall employee strength initially was around eight to ten, including Mr Lokhande and Mr Shinde. Interestingly both had mastered the skills of preparing CAD/CAM software during their service earlier and had no hesitation in investing in hardware for such programs as well.

Launch and Growth Phase

Starting with a turnover of just around Rs 30–40 lakhs in the year 2007–2008, PDE has never looked back. PDE has added four to five major customers every year, with repeat orders from these customers every year since 2009. As much as the requirements became unique and challenging, PDE has stretched its limits each time to bag the new type of requirements from existing and new customers. Both Mr Lokhande and Mr Shinde were busy during this period visiting Machine Tool Exhibitions in India and abroad and meeting foreign collaborators of their Indian customers to understand and prepare for future requirements with changed designs and technology.

The growth momentum of PDE has helped their customers, especially major automobile companies, to localize their requirements on PDE for components parts and assembly for their new products and improvements in the existing products. In a way, PDE has been an important factor in auto companies deciding to develop new products for and in India and save both time and dear foreign currency by having their prototype requirements met by PDE.

PDE, deciding strategically to expand their boundaries in 2012, invested and established a new process facility with an additional investment of nearly Rs 5 crores of modernization in precision machinery and replacing old machines with new technology and adequate capability building in the design and manufacture of soft tooling requires for prototypes. Another important headway was to supply in small and medium quantities even the components developed as prototypes for the initial product launch program of the automobile companies. One can only imagine the huge amount of financial and schedule support this provides to the final customer in ease of introducing new products against the severe competition in the market. This was like a feather in the cap of PDE by adding to its competitive advantage position with respect to competition.

Another milestone of 2012, PDE added a new partner to the company, Mr Sumit Bagrecha, to expand the firm's activities to the global market. Sumit is a well-qualified young engineer from sound family background, done his MSc from Berlin University in Germany and has a good command of the German language.

The intention of including Sumit on board as a partner has come true, and now PDE is a global supplier of prototype parts to German Auto Manufacturers as well.

Between 2013 and 2016, understanding the importance of nearness to market, PDE has established plants with manufacturing facilities at Chennai and Jamshedpur in addition to the existing two in Pune, the nerve centres of the auto industry in India—the total investments in plant and machinery has crossed 30 crore mark and is asking for more.

The turnover starting from a few lakhs in 2008 is currently hovering around Rs 65 crores and if one has to list the amount of foreign exchange saved by auto companies due to the supply support from PDE, it will be mind-boggling and is a true Make in India contribution from PDE.

The organization:	Proto D Engineering—MIDC Chakan, Pune
Managing partners:	Responsible for all major investment and strategic plans
1. Mr Dipak Shinde Dipl. Digital Electronics	Primarily responsible for price and delivery negotiations
2. Mr Pradip Lokhande Dipl. Production technology	Primarily responsible for procurement and plant utilization
3. Mr Sumitkumar Bagrecha B.E. Mechanical; MSc. Global Prodn Engg., Germany	Primarily responsible for new markets and customer contacts
Operative engineers and workforce	10 Engineers + 45 regular operators

Major Strategic Growth Plans

Diversify the customer segment from automobiles to the infrastructure and construction sector:

India Railways and material handling equipment (BEML, IR)
Defence equipment prototype manufacture (DRDO)
Market segments in Europe and Latin America

Accreditations and Testimonials

CRISIL

Rating SE2B (valid till 2017)—high-performance capability and moderate financial strength—good stability and strong profitability.

ISO 9001-2008 certified (*TUV* Ford)

SMERA rating MSME 3 (above average)

Appreciation letters from M&M Ltd, Tata Motors, and other OE customers are measures of Confidence the OE customers have on Proto D Engineering Pvt LTD.

Case Questions

1. What strategy do you propose for PDE for scaling up the organization to achieve a turnover target of Rs 100 crores by 2018?

2. What business model do you suggest for PDE for long-range growth and business sustainability?

3. Should PDE look to set up branch factories abroad, especially in Latin America and Mexico?

4. Can the boutique concept be used by PDE for the promotion of its production capability and market growth?

3

Corporate Governance under Threat?

Tale of Two Titans

Learning Objectives

The world over today, compliance to corporate governance (CG) norms has been a prerequisite in all business transactions, from normal vendor certification to the distributor agreements and more in particular to domestic and international mergers and acquisitions. In many instances, non-compliance to laid down CG practices has been a major contention and a cause for major boardroom conflicts.

This has made the set of new CEOs to suspect the very motives of the erstwhile founders misusing the CG as a tool to suppress the new leadership and reminder them to respect the real power centres at the founders' disposal.

Hence a time is ripe now to revisit the restrictive adherence to CG to the extent that the new leaders have an elbow room to steer the organization to face global completion supported by certain flexibility needed without of course drifting from the core values of the organization.

This case study takes the reader through such tricky situations that the new class leadership is trying to win over.

Synopsis

The Tatas and Infosys of India two are iconic names. They command enormous brand equity. They had been in the news for all the wrong reasons. The happenings at Tata Sons and Infosys have brought the focus

Indian Business Case Studies. Srilatha Palekar, Arun Pardhi and Sunanda Jindal, Oxford University Press. © ASM Group of Institutes, Pune, India 2022. DOI: 10.1093/oso/9780192869449.003.0003

firmly on CG. Some may call them board-room tussles. Others may view them as owners-versus-the-board fight.

The question is: Have these episodes hurt governance in these organizations?

In both instances, owners or the founders (Ratan Tata in Tata Sons and N.R. Narayana Murthy in Infosys) were in the eye of a storm. While the Tata board was run by a mix of promoters-cum-professionals, Infosys founders had left it to professionals to run the show. At Bombay House, it all started with the ouster of Cyrus Mistry as the chairman, resulting in Mr. Tata taking over as the interim chairman of Tata Sons. The development led to a slew of allegations and counter-allegations. Questions were raised on the way business had been run and certain strategic decisions made. The Mistry-Tata battle also reached court-rooms. In the case of Infosys, Mr. Murthy flagged issues involving higher compensation to executives, acquisition strategy, and appointment of independent directors. He publicly expressed unhappiness over the current management. In the case of Tatas, they chose to re-move Mr. Mistry.

At Tata Sons, the controlling shareholder (Tata Trusts, which own 68% stake) had lost faith in its chairman to lead the group and subsequently replaced him. In Infosys, the founders own only 13% stake. Still, they expressed dissent.

After an ugly fracas, N. Chandrasekaran has taken over as Tata Sons chairman. His elevation has been smooth. There are signs of the group looking to resolve many a contentious issue that dominated the headlines in the wake of the Mistry-Tata fight. The group's cash cow TCS has announced a ₹16,000-crore share buy-back programme. Tata Sons has indicated that it would also participate.

The funds thus obtained would help pare its debts. Tata Sons also has worked out a settlement with DoCoMo, which was one of the key friction points between Mr. Tata and Mr. Mistry. All the subsequent events have been very smooth with almost the entire shareholding community supporting the promoter's initiatives. It is also a happy ending to one of the major controversies with DoCoMo. The way the settlement is being done indicates clearly Mr. Tata's ways of doing business. At Infosys, the board was quick to clarify issues raised by the promoters.

Targets Differ

There is a crucial difference between these two episodes, however. In the case of Tata Sons, the target was the chairman, Mr. Mistry. At Infosys, the whole board and, by inference, the senior management, were the targets for the founders. The Tata issue turned legal because there was definite action by the controlling shareholder. In Infosys, it was about the founders expressing their dissent on certain decisions taken by the board.

Do the owners or founders have the right or obligation to an organization that they have assiduously built over many summers? More precisely, can the board or management just brush aside the view of a 'quality shareholder' (Mr. Tata and Mr. Murthy in these instances)?

It is never in doubt that Mr. Tata is a globally revered name. It is also well known than Mr. Murthy is the password for India in gaining global recognition. Events at the Tata empire have subsequently proved that shareholder supremacy prevails in the end. The succession at Tata Sons has turned out to be a smooth affair, and the operating companies did not see any performance dislocation in those troubled times.

Analysts also point to a core difference between these two cases. In the case of Tata Sons, the owner and quality shareholder (read Mr. Tata) was pitched against a chairman (read Mr. Mistry).

In Infosys, Narayana Murthy-led founders were largely responsible for professionalizing the organization right from the time of inception. The current professional management headed by R. Seshasayee, not surprisingly, felt no constraint in admitting to their misjudgement, if any, and papering over their differences with the founders who are professionals in their own right.

According to S. Santhanakrishnan, an expert on corporate law and governance and also a director on the board of Tata Global Beverages, CG has succeeded in both instances.

While the issues were handled differently, what is to be appreciated is how quickly the problems were resolved. Infosys board was quick to address issues raised by the founders. At Tatas, the leader had to be replaced because of lack of confidence.

'It is also further strengthened by the fact that shareholders have full faith in Tata's name and brand and all stakeholders including stock markets have veered positively, at the end, towards the Tata group, that the differing methodologies pursued in these instances should be under-stood in the context of targets of founders and owners.

There is a lesson to be learnt from these episodes. The trust of the shareholders—more so that of quality shareholders—can never be wished away'.

Infosys Board vs Narayana Murthy: Is the Fight Really Over?

Conciliatory remarks by N.R. Narayana Murthy, flattering ones about Murthy and Infosys Ltd by Vishal Sikka, and reassurances by the always-proper R. Seshasayee that everyone was on the same side seemed to suggest on Monday that India's second largest software services firm had put the tussle between founders, board, and management behind it. But is it really over?

Sikka, the first professional CEO of the company founded by Murthy and six others in 1981, and Seshasayee, a well-regarded professional manager and current chairman of the company, insisted in an interview that it was. 'I cannot assure you anything, but me and Mr Murthy have spoken, and I hope something like this doesn't happen again', said Seshasayee.

Murthy, called Seshasayee a man of 'highest integrity', and indicated that he had pretty much said what he wanted to and was confident the company would address the issues. Sikka said his relationship with the founders 'is wonderful'. He added that 'it is a real privilege' to be Infosys' leader. Seshasayee and Sikka said Infosys' board continues to 'address issues all stakeholders, including ones that the founders have'. Seshasayee clarified that these issues would be addressed by the board 'within the overall framework of the fiduciary responsibility it has to all shareholders'.

He added that there is no 'negotiated compromise formula' and that the board would treat the promoters just as it does 'any other share-holders'. He said he has been entrusted with a job to do by the company and had no intention of leaving unless he is asked to. 'Here we have some stakeholders, founders and others along with them, who have nothing other than the best interest of the organization on their mind and obviously, there will be a lot of passion', Seshasayee said.

That isn't the clear message analysts were expecting to hear, although it may be all they get. 'I believe both parties (founders and the board) have realized that there has to be some compromise, meaning some demands of the founders met, and at the same time letting the current board and management run it the way they want', said a Mumbai-based analyst at a foreign brokerage after the press conference (ET prime). 'But the most surprising thing is that looking at the commentary from the press conference, we do not know if that compromise has been reached.' The analyst requested anonymity.

Murthy's main issues with the board were over the severance pay to former chief financial officer Rajiv Bansal (that was subsequently stopped, last year itself, after Murthy expressed his displeasure) and the increase in CEO Sikka's salary by 55% to $11 million a year. On Monday, Seshasayee said the first issue had taught the board to remove subjectivity about severance pay and insert it in employment contracts. He also defended Sikka's pay and said it was approved by the board and shareholders.

Murthy's comments in recent days have caused a stir, with many experts and analysts drawing parallels with recent events in the Tata group, where Cyrus Mistry was fired as chairman of holding company Tata Sons Ltd on 24 October last year and evicted from the board on 6 February 2016.

When Performance Becomes More Important Than Values: Wells Fargo

It is difficult to open a newspaper without seeing the latest on the Tata Sons vs. Cyrus Mistry conflict. Based on the information that has been covered so far, it is clear that there came a point where the core values of the company were pushed aside in favour of performance. The emotional disconnection with the values of a company starts at the board level and trickles down to management and lower-level employees—this is likely what led to the conflict and trust deficit between the Tata Trust and Mr Cyrus Mistry, the ex-chairman of Tata Sons on 24 October 2016.

So, let's talk about emotional connection and values vs. the fear for performance. As a board member with a fiduciary responsibility to shareholders, it is easy to say performance is the most important part of your role, but the truth is that performance should be closely tied to emotional connection and values. The emotional connection serves as the foundation for emotional safety. It is basically what gives board members safety when they have to work together. Values are what keeps the board on track.

The emotional connection to each other and the company allows the brain to stay calm and remain connected even in times of great stress. When we don't pay attention to the emotional connection, we get disconnected and slowly move away from values. Our brains lose the safety of the group. Decisions become inconsistent, and panic sets in to protect self-interest becomes prevalent in the boardroom. All of this leads to poor performance. But when the brain is emotionally connected, we see better collaboration, more creativity, and better ideas, which of course leads to better overall performance.

The way the board treats the emotional connection guides how the executive team approaches the values, which moves down to management and all the way down to frontline employees. When the board is disconnected, it loses sight of the mission, vision, and values, so does everyone else.

Emotional disconnection is often driven by fear. There are certain basic fears that come up in all relationships—fear of abandonment and fear of rejection. If we look at fear that led Wells Fargo to the decision of committing fraud, there were four different relationships that were impacted by fear:

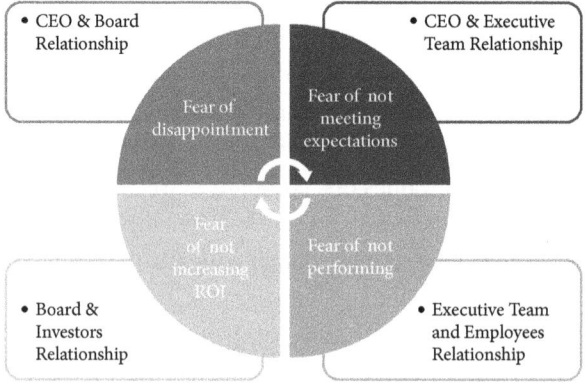

Relations Matrix for the CEOs

Wanting to stay connected by pleasing everyone is a natural part of being human. The fear of not meeting expectations often what get CEOs in trouble because they don't know how to address their emotion with the board and the board does not know how to help them deal with that fear. Thus, CEOs obsession for performance turns into a tunnel vision— ignoring the values and emotional disconnection with the board. This laser-like focus almost always ends poorly for the company.

In the case of the Tatas & Mistry, performance became the focal point. With terms like 'Managing through Shambles', it is easy to see how focus got turned from their values which include 'Managing by Trust' to 'what's right for me' performance.

The tragedy in all of this is that performance obsession happens to so many boards, and it is so hard for them to see it as it is happening. So how can you stop this from happening on your board? Or better yet, how can you tell if this is currently happening on your board? It's simple—bring it back to emotional connection. Ask your fellow board members if they can share their concerns openly and honestly on the board. Have a candid conversation about if and how you can create safety so that you can refer to values when making decisions. Ask your management if they know the values—chances are if they are not familiar with the values, neither are your frontline employees.

If it is apparent that there is a disconnect between the people and the values, take some time to review. Do the values need to be changed? If you are not using the values, how are you making decisions? The most important part of this conversation is to reconnect the board emotionally with the company.

Remind everyone why they joined the board in the first place—they care about the company and want it to succeed. Implementing values and speaking about them regularly is one of the best ways to maintain that emotional connection and prevent performance pressures from taking over.

What we can really learn from the Tatas Conflict is that even if you have a strong and competent board, it is all easily lost when fear and disconnection are introduced into the boardroom. Competence turns into incompetence and things that should be obvious are ignored or pushed aside as directors, CEOs, managers, and frontline employees stop focusing on the company's values and start doing everything they can to protect themselves. Learning, understanding, and knowing how to work with emotion becomes essential in developing a culture where people feel safe and connected to protect the company together.

Case Questions

1. Both the Tata Group and Infosys are the real creators and practioners of Corporate Governance as an essential feature ans aspect of Ethically and Rationally managed organisations. In fact both these organisations are the initiators of Corporate Governance Implementation in major Industrial Organisations. If this be so how is that major hiccups challenging the compliance to CG also begin at the back yard of these very organisations i.e. Tatas and Infosys Ltd?

2. On a plane reading and understanding of issues at Tatas and Infosys, it appears that both the parties involved are right through their own interpretations Could these issues smell of personal egos playing a major role than the reasoning put forth by all involved in the Board room battle at Tas and Infosys?

3. What in your view the final observation? (Please list down few of your major observations.) Except that two senior board level Members have been shunted out but nothing has changed in the way both businesses are being managed except change of Guards.

4

Transformational Leadership

A Case Study in Strategic HR

Learning Objectives

The real business transformations so essential for business sustainability and survival in present-day Volatile Uncertain Complex Ambiguous (VUCA) at marketplaces appears only feasible if the top management is committed to envision, enabling, and enacting responsibilities it has to accept and lead the business transformational efforts from the front.

Many organizations have made it farcical by appointing global change management consultants and at the end got back only to realize that not much has changed at the ground level in some cases causing damage to better ways of conducting business operation followed earlier. There are many such examples of failed organizational transformation efforts more so due to remote management and control approach.

However, there are certain oasis type situations wherein one sometimes cannot comprehend the extent of desired strategic change brought about by committed leaderships of such organizations Mahindra & Mahindra Ltd the largest Tractor manufacturers globally and market leaders in Indian SUV segment along with Bharat Forge (Kalyani Group of Industries) are flag bearers of bringing about such organizational transformations.

The case study takes the reader through all that matters for a successful business transformation project.

Indian Business Case Studies. Srilatha Palekar, Arun Pardhi and Sunanda Jindal, Oxford University Press. © ASM Group of Institutes, Pune, India 2022. DOI: 10.1093/oso/9780192869449.003.0004

Synopsis

Through the group's state of the art engineering centre in Pune, India Bharat Forge Limited (BFL), an Indian multinational company in the private sector is able to provide comprehensive product design capabilities to enable significantly lower 'time-to-market' for its customers Original Equipment (OE). With its long-standing expertise in automotive components, Bharat Forge Group has been providing customers with a complete range of product design, analysis, prototyping, and testing service.

India-based BFL is globally the second largest auto forging company after ThyssenKrupp of Germany. BFL is the flagship company of Pune- based Kalyani Group with interests in steel, steel-based products, forgings, and automotive components. The company made a humble beginning in 1961 with a small plant in Pune. Over the years, the company has become the second-largest auto forging company, globally the second largest engine component manufacturer.

Along with manufacturing forging items and components for automobiles and commercial vehicles, the company was also a global leader in producing components for railways, earth moving equipment, hydrocarbons, sugar, steel, coal, shipbuilding, oil and gas, refinery, and general engineering equipment. Globally, BFL is known for its operational excellence, technical supremacy, and cutting-edge know-how.

It has an enviable buyers list from global automotive companies like, General Motors, DaimlerChrysler, Volvo, Mitsubishi Corporation, Toyota Motor Corporation, and Hyundai Motors. It also had tie-ups, joint ventures, and technology sharing with leading auto component manufacturers and original equipment manufacturers like Meritor, Carpenter Technology Corporation, Rockwell International, and Delphi Corporation. As a part of the growth strategy, the company opted for both green-field expansion and brown-field expansion. BFL has made a few significant acquisitions globally to mark its presence. Among the list of the acquisitions, Carl Dan Peddinghaus, CDP Aluminium Technik, and Imatra Kilsta AB are the most significant ones.

Through this case study, it is intended to discuss in detail about how the SHR strategy has facilitated the company to become a global leader in the auto forging industry. In view of its management philosophy,

Organisational Development (OD) Strategy enabling it to become a global leader. The case study focuses on the HR model of the company and glimpses of the employer branding exercises of Kalyani Group, its unique leadership style, Its HR branding, balanced score card on performance evaluation, performance ethics quality of work life, employee retention, etc.

This case further offers a scope for discussion about the HR policy trends and strategy of the industry, the CSR strategy adopted by the company; the limitations and scope of the HR strategies in the company.

The Case

Part of Kalyani Group—a US$ 2.5 billion conglomerate with a 10,000 global workforce; BFL today has the largest repository of metallurgical knowledge in the region and offers full-service supply capability to its global marquee customers from conceptualization to product design, engineering, manufacturing, testing, and validation. An annual total turnover of Rs. 1000–2500 crores and with employee strength of 5001 and above in Pune unit.

Innovation has been the driving force behind the company and is applied across every aspect of the business. Their R&D team has been working on various projects, including developing technologies to minimizing carbon footprint and producing lightweight products which translate into lower energy consumption. The auto world is moving to a greener, fossil-free technology. They have tied up with like-minded companies to develop technology that our automotive clientele can capitalize on.

The company has been focusing sharply on innovating in the automotive space with new technology and products while continuing to explore opportunities in the non-automotive space. The innovative application of the latest technologies has helped the company develop critical, high value, high value-added products for the non-automotive sector. Today BFL is an indigenous supply source for some of these products, which were largely imported.

Guided by the visionary leadership of Dr B. N. Kalyani, Group chairman, with a strong emphasis on market leadership through technology, the group today is a market leader in all its respective business segments.

- Largest forging company in the world
- No. 1 in engineering steel in India
- No. 1 in axle aggregates in India

Dr Baba Kalyani is the Chairman of the Kalyani Group of companies and chairman and managing director of the group's flagship—BFL—India's large manufacturer and exporter of automotive components. No. 1 Indian exporter of wheels.

Brains, Not Muscles

Bharat Forge was founded in 1961, during the heyday of Nehruvian socialism in India. At the time, central planning and import substitution were pillars of Indian economic policy. Although state-owned industries were encouraged to control the so-called commanding heights of the economy, the private sector was never entirely shut out. The firm, recalls the Kalyani group, was formed to serve two somewhat disparate markets—diesel engines used by farmers for irrigation and a nascent domestic auto industry. 'It was mainly buses and trucks', says Kalyani. 'In those days, the passenger car market was very small' (BS News Paper). At any rate, both irrigation and automobiles required engines, and engines required parts. Bharat Forge arranged for technical assistance from a firm in Cleveland, Ohio. The Kalyanis also had close family ties with some of the region's leading industrial houses, such as the Kirloskars and Tatas, which were among Bharat Forge's first customers.

Over the next three decades, India persevered with its brand of socialism even as Asian tigers such as Korea and Taiwan leap-frogged to prosperity powered by industrialization and exports. For Bharat Forge, this was a time of consolidation within India's protected domestic market. It focused on technology and quality and carved out a reputation for reliability. Then in 1988, not so long before India embarked upon economic reforms, Bharat Forge decided to take a big gamble: Realizing that it was not possible to achieve economies of scale with a relatively low technology and low-skilled workforce, it invested one billion rupees (at the time, turnover was only Rs. 1.5 billion) in a sophisticated German-engineered plant. 'We decided to bet the house on technology', says Kalyani.

Along with the investment in technology came an upgrade of manpower. Traditionally, Bharat Forge, like other Indian firms, had employed a poorly educated workforce often virtually indistinguishable from farm labour. Now it began the process of replacing them with the kind of educated workers who would be able to make the most of the new technology. Through a combination of attractive severance packages and attrition, a third of the firm's 1,800-strong workforce was replaced. By the time the transition was completed, a largely blue-collar factory floor had become largely white-collar.

Today, Bharat Forge employs about 4,000 people, but 80% of them are college graduates, and a third are qualified engineers. 'These are extremely bright, fast and hardworking people. They have good values', says Kalyani. 'We needed computing and analytical skills which the blue collar guys just didn't have. For the company this was a cultural change. We replaced muscle power with brain power' (BS News Paper).

In retrospect, the decision seems obvious, but at the time, it was seen as risky. Arindam Bhattacharya, a New Delhi-based BCG director, credits Bharat Forge chairman B.N. Kalyani with the foresight. 'What sets them apart is that in Baba Kalyani they have an outstanding leader', says Bhattacharya. 'He's ambitious, but also an outstanding technical person with a very deep knowledge of tool design. He's been the key factor in increasing productivity. They have gone against the grain, which was to use labor costs for competitive advantage. They are able to get the most out of their machines' (BS News Paper).

In 1991, India began opening its economy to competition and foreign capital. The country's auto parts manufacturers moved to upgrade their technology and skills, accelerating a process that had begun with the government-owned Maruti Udyog's co-production of a small car with Japanese auto manufacturer Suzuki in 1983. Keeping with Japanese practice, Suzuki's suppliers in Japan had followed it to India and played a large role in technology transfer and training. After liberalization, India's potentially vast domestic market attracted a raft of auto companies. Toyota, Hyundai, and Ford manufacture cars in India and source parts from Indian suppliers.

Dr Baba Kalyani—A Transformative Leader

Dr Baba N. Kalyani, Chairman, Kalyani Group was honoured with the much-coveted 'Lifetime Achievement Award' at the Asian Business Leadership Forum's award ceremony in Abu Dhabi on 27th November 2012.

The ABLF Lifetime Achievement Award is awarded to people who wield immense influence to mentor a generation of business leaders with old-world wisdom and sharp business acumen and who consistently place team, community, and country on his/her lead agenda. The ABLF Awards Grand Jury consists of a high-profile group of eminent industry experts, economic commentators, and international leaders from government, business, academics, advisory, and other professional disciplines.

Baba Kalyani holds an MS in Engineering from Massachusetts Institute of Technology, United States. He is the chairman and managing director of the Kalyani Group of companies. He serves on the boards of many prestigious companies and represents the industry on several industry, trade, and educational institutions in India and abroad. 'PADMA BHUSHAN', one of the most distinguished civilian awards by the Government of India for his contributions to trade and industry.

Mr Kalyani serves on the boards of many prestigious companies and represents industry on several industry, trade, and educational institutions in India and abroad. Notable amongst these are the National Manufacturing Competitiveness Council (NMCC) and the National Knowledge Commission (NKC).

Mr Kalyani is the founder chairman of Pratham Pune Education Foundation, an NGO that is engaged in providing primary education to children belonging to underprivileged sections of the local community. Since its inception in 2000, Pratham Pune has made a difference in the lives of over 100,000 children in Pune society. Mr. Kalyani is also steering a unique initiative to empower rural youth at a Taluka in Pune district by providing free technical and vocational training at a government Industrial Training Institute (ITI) that is being run as a public–private partnership. The pioneering model is being replicated in other parts of the country. Mr. Kalyani also supports various other NGOs and charitable institutes engaged in education and in uplifting the quality of lives of the disadvantaged and needy.

In pursuance of his vision to contribute to a clean and emission-free environment, Mr Kalyani has set up a new venture Kenersys Limited to manufacture various energy-efficient wind turbines for domestic and international markets. The company also has its own wind turbines in Maharashtra, which generate 'green energy' for the group's manufacturing operations. Mr Kalyani is also engaged in developing solar energy equipment that would contribute to further strengthening his group's footprint in the non-conventional energy sector. In a joint venture with KPIT Cummins, Bharat Forge is developing a unique hybrid solution that would contribute to the country being able to meet its vehicular emission targets.

'Doctor of Science' (honoris causa) by IIT Kharagpur for his outstanding contribution to entrepreneurship and for making Bharat Forge a global leader in the forging industry,

'Cross of the Order of Merit', the highest honour awarded to individuals for their admirable services to the Federal Republic of Germany,

'COMMANDER FIRST CLASS' of the 'ROYAL ORDER OF THE POLAR STAR' by the Swedish government in recognition of his contribution in furthering trade and Business cooperation between Sweden and India,

Global Economy Prize 2009 for business by Kiel Institute, German 'Businessman of the Year-2006' by Business India Magazine,

'Entrepreneur of the Year 2005 for Manufacturing' by Ernst & Young and 'CEO of the Year 2004' by the Business Standard.

The spirit of innovation is the credo of Baba Kalyani's organization. He reiterates, the company mission as to 'be committed to listening and responding to the needs of customers, associates and business partners and to be committed to growing along with employees and to aid and encourage them to participate in the goals in order that they realize their full potential'.

Their historical success is directly related to a combination of skills and competencies of managerial team and highly qualified and motivated talent pool. The process of transformation into a global company presents a new challenge for Bharat Forge—that of building world-class human resources. In fact, this has been one of the key priorities for the company over the last few years. Based on practices followed at their German operations, they have started an apprentice training program at Pune where new recruits at the shop floor level are being continuously mentored for 18 months by a senior engineer or executive. This not only quickly familiarizes the recruits with the company's technologies and best practices but also gives management the opportunity to identify high potential talent.

They have an arrangement with BITS, Pilani through which Bharat Forge employees can pursue a three-year part-time engineering course. There have been 40 successful candidates in the first batch and will commence an expanded second batch of 48 in early August 2013. In addition to this, they are also taking steps to develop a 'talent pool' of essential engineering skillsets through a well-structured process of creating 'Master Engineers'. This initiative has resulted in BFL having gained Competitive Advantage position amongst its competitors which helps them major difference and infrastructure contracts from Government of India (GOI).

BFL has also initiated structured 'Leadership Development' programs for senior management as means to create global managers—people who can operate across borders with confidence, deal with the diversity of cultures, and be highly analytical and result-oriented.

'The test of a first class mind is the ability to hold two opposing ideas in the mind simultaneously, and yet be able to function.'—this is the quality that differentiates a good manager from an exceptional one and which BFL are trying to develop their management team (BS News Paper).

BFL was using an outdated automated system to manage its diverse workforce. The system required employees to perform many tasks manually, which negatively affected productivity and payroll accuracy. BFL chose a Kronos® solution because it provided complete automation and would help significantly cut down on the extensive time taken for payroll processing. Since the implementation of the Kronos Workforce Central® suite, not only has Bharat Forge managed to dramatically reduce the amount of time it takes to process payroll, but the company also has achieved more accurate processing and increased productivity. The integrated suite proved to be a wise investment, helping BFL perform and there was no modernization with Workforce Central suite leads to new efficiencies.

By implementing the Kronos Workforce Central suite with its powerful Workforce Timekeeper application, Bharat Forge was finally able to successfully address its existing challenges—and more. With this comprehensive time and attendance solution in place, the company was able to eliminate more than 6,000 manual leave cards, remove outdated time clocks, and deploy self-service capabilities to every employee.

The Kronos implementation also empowered managers to conduct many tasks online, such as viewing and approving employee timecards, leave cards, OD cards, and short leave requests. This significantly reduced the number of manual payroll entries and checks, and increased employee satisfaction.

Empowered Employees and Managers Enjoy New Access

The ability to view employee time, leave, on-premise reports, and other critical information in real-time proved to be very beneficial. Managers were relieved of the burden of completing manual timesheets and other records, and enjoyed other capabilities that were not previously available. With Kronos, they now had online access to real-time on-premise reports; exception reports such as data on absenteeism, late in/early out, and overtime; and more.

Employee Satisfaction Increases with Self-Service

Every major change in the process takes some getting used to. For Bharat Forge, getting all employees to utilize the new self-service system was easier because acceptance went from the top down. All employees in the company use Kronos to record their time worked, access leave balances, apply for leave, and view other relevant time and attendance information. All these functionalities were available for BFL employees to access in the production bay on self-service kiosks (terminals), which also record their attendance. As a result, employee satisfaction and productivity went up, since employees no longer needed to report to the time office to access or record their information.

In response to global customers' preference for suppliers to have technology centres close to their product development facilities, they have set up a product design and engineering facility in Germany. This will enable them to leverage the high technology skills available at our German operations to deepen customer relationships and pursue our quest for global technology leadership. We will build up strong design and engineering capabilities at each of our global locations in order to provide our customers with the highest level of service and support.

Corporate Social Responsibility

There is a significant increase in the expectations of a wide range of stakeholders—customers, employees, investors, communities, and governments—in regard to a company's commitment to socially responsible business practices. As a result, corporate social responsibility is becoming a progressively more important component of good business practice.

Bharat Forge is proud of being a socially committed organization and a responsible corporate citizen. BFL attaches greater importance to discharging our responsibilities to the community and society where we are located.

Our major focus is on supporting pre-school and primary education with an emphasis on children in the local community in the age group of 3–14 belonging to underprivileged sections of society. For the past five years, Kalyani Group companies have been supporting Pratham Pune Education Foundation, an NGO that is engaged in this activity.

Pratham has so far touched the lives of over 50,000 children and has contributed to improving their prospects for a better future. While Dr Kalyani personally initiated Pratham's activities in Pune, partners include a few of the city's leading corporate houses, the Pune Municipal Corporation and GE Foundation, United States, who are generously supporting this worthy cause.

Besides Pratham, they also support other NGOs that are engaged in various social activities targeted to benefit the community at large. For our employees and their families, we run a community centre whose focus is to spread greater awareness and understanding about issues concerning children's education, health, women's welfare, and environmental concerns.

Training of Manpower

Along with the investment in technology came an upgrade of manpower. Traditionally, Bharat Forge, like other Indian firms, had employed a poorly educated workforce often virtually indistinguishable from farm labour. Now it began the process of replacing them with the kind of educated workers who would be able to make the most of the new technology. Through a combination of attractive severance packages and attrition a third of the firm's 1,800-strong workforce was replaced. By the time the transition was completed, a largely blue-collar factory floor had become largely white collar.

Today, Bharat Forge employs about 4,000 people, but 80% of them are college graduates and a third are engineers. 'These are extremely bright, fast and hardworking people. They have good values,' says Kalyani. 'We needed computing and analytical skills which the blue collar guys just didn't have. For the company this was a cultural change. We replaced muscle power with brain power.'

Caging the demon of economic crises: The solid HR administration with concern for productivity combined with innovation-based far-sighted approach has yielded significant results both in top-line and bottom-line performance of the company.

In 2006, Bharat Forge had total sales of US$659 million and had a market value of US$1.8 billion. It was rated as one of the best companies in Asia by the *Forbes* magazine because of its high growth rate. The company increased its sales by more than 50% in 2005. In FY2006, BFL set out on a new growth path where it focused on aggressively developing its industrial sector components business and chalked out a large investment plan to develop dedicated facilities in Baramati, Satara, and Pune.

In the automotive forgings business, it planned to further grow and consolidate its position by increasing its customer base and penetrating deeper into global markets through its Indian and overseas operations.

However, the company was severely impacted by the global economic turmoil in 2008. BFL responded to the market adversities by looking inwards and reorienting its business focus. The company recalibrated its business strategy and focused on streamlining operations to create a leaner and more cost-efficient enterprise that could generate profits by operating at lower levels of capacity utilization. And, in FY2011, with much of the strategic initiatives of FY2006 and the restructuring post-2008 firmly in place, Bharat Forge leveraged the revival across its target markets to deliver strong results across its business platforms.

Case Questions

1. Does the HR policy of the company support the philosophy that investment in the right direction is the key to harnessing profit, not cost-cutting?

2. Bharat Forge is a name to reckon in independent India's success stories in family-managed businesses. The group today is almost a pioneer in entering difficult businesses like defence and has gone out across the world for lucrative Investment opportunities. It is really paradoxical that such a progressive group is often hampered by frequent IR issues. What could be a few priority aspects which should be focused on by the management to establish a cordial IR climate in its businesses?

5

Dishends Pvt Ltd

A Case Study on HR/IR Issues in an SME Enterprise

Learning Objectives

Among the major obstacles to managing smooth operations in small and medium type organizations run by entrepreneurs who have just succeeded in establishing their capabilities in the market as reliable suppliers of goods and services deemed so necessary for major manufacturers are perennial disturbed IR situations.

It is a real balancing issue for the promoters to have patience, energy, and financial strength to deal effectively with such IR nuisances all along. The situations get complicated especially when an outside union leader is able to get a leadership role for negotiating issues on wage and amenities who at times play highly destructive and demonizing role to mislead the employees even to disregard their own and family interests and become victims and perpetuators of violence and long-term disturbance/stoppage of operations.

The IR laws provide for such outside union interventions as legally permissible, further complicating the negotiations through protracted labour court proceedings which in many cases have led to permanent closure of many such small- and medium-sized units.

For the students of HR, the case study provides an excellent insight into such situations in normally smooth sailing business operations in SMEs.

Synopsis

Managing small enterprises has always been an issue in compliance with all regulatory acts as also the company's and industrial disputes act. The

Indian Business Case Studies. Srilatha Palekar, Arun Pardhi and Sunanda Jindal, Oxford University Press. © ASM Group of Institutes, Pune, India 2022. DOI: 10.1093/oso/9780192869449.003.0005

entrepreneur with all the resources at his commend tries to maintain his business in spite of major issues in working capital management.

The main issue also is the IR climate in spite of the fact that most of the small entrepreneurs work with their own hands along with their employees' frequent issues such as payment of wages, bonuses, and annual increments or renewal of union agreements cause major disturbance to smooth running of the unit.

Dishends

The case study provides an insight as to how an entrepreneur and his partners struggle hard to manage a business with such IR issues.

Mr Mohanlal Yadav, an engineer with experience from Rohtaj industries, founded the Dishends Ltd in 1975 at Thane–Belapur Road, Navi Mumbai. The management was formed by four engineers, including Mr Mohanlal Yadav. It was the manufacturing of vessels of MS, SS material required for pharmaceutical, chemical companies, fertilizers companies' large government and private enterprises like HOC, NOCIL, Hardllia Chemicals, Standard Alkalie, and other dairy and pharmacy companies.

They were manufacturing dish-ends required for diesel petrol tankers. It was a quality product for which they employed highly skilled employees, supervisors, and engineers. The total strength of the company was more than 500 workers. The company was working in three shifts. It was headed by well-qualified top management.

In 1978, workers formed a union under the leadership of S.R. Kanitkar, who was the leader of workers of chemical and pharmaceutical companies in the Thane belt. His asset was that he was an advocate dealing with industrial dispute cases. From the company, there were two three local workers who were interested in forming a union and especially Mr Ramesh from the machine shop who took the lead and met Mr S.R. Kanitkar and proposed that under his leadership a workers union at Dishends Ltd can be established.

They registered this union under the heading of Dishends Employees Union and submitted a letter to the company under the presidentship of S.R. Kanitkar. Most of the workers joined this union called General Chemical Workers Union and informed the management that the union wanted to negotiate the demands of the workers. The matter was not taken up seriously by the management and it lingered till 1980.

In the meantime, Mr S. K. Jadhav, a widely experienced personnel manager with having a good understanding of the complexity of industrial relations, joined the company as its first personnel manager.

Due to the financial crisis, this company was not in a position to consider the demands of the workers and it was many times informed to the union unit committee. During the period of meetings with the unit committee, it was observed by the management that the committee was not cooperative and was adamant during the negotiations.

The union had put up a charter of demands with 25 items. Its major demand was a rise in the wages of all the workmen in basic and dearness allowance of Rs. 1,500 per month. Other demands were related to an increase in incentives, bonuses, uniforms, increase in LTA, free facilities for transportation, education allowance, HRA, etc.

The management, for all the times during the meetings, was trying to convince the committee members of the financial constraints of the company. The leadership was from the local area and no one was able to understand the total financial implications against the demands which were placed before the management.

The workers were getting impatient, as only the negotiations were going on and the issues were prolonged. In December 1979, Ramesh, a local leader, with the help of political parties, started pressuring the management, to fulfil their demands as per their charter of demands. The management called a meeting with the President of the union, Mr S.R. Kanitkar, wherein they tried to explain to him the company's financial crisis and requested to maintain peace in the company as workers were unnecessarily creating unrest without understanding the management's problems.

In the meeting itself, S.R. Kanitkar advised the committee members to maintain peace in the company so that negotiations could proceed further. In the said meeting, Ramesh and other committee members did not say anything and went out from the meeting. Both management and Trade Union leaders were unhappy with the attitude of the committee members.

In the month of January 1980, gradually labour unrest increased and the activities of the workmen because of instigation from committee members became non-cooperative. They started threatening the supervisors, which adversely affected production activities.

One of the supervisors of second shift, Mr Nair was abused and threatened by Mr Ramesh related to the pending demands. Mr Nair tried to convince him and requested him not to become violent. Instead of listening to him, Mr Ramesh slapped Mr. Nair in the presence of the workmen who were on duty in the second shift on 10 January 1980.

Mr Nair reported this matter to the management in writing the next morning. On the same day, i.e. 11 January 1980, the personnel manager, Mr S.K. Jadhav had been to Thane Police Station along with a letter related with factory matters to be informed to ACP Thane. After returning from Thane, as Mr S. K. Jadhav was walking towards factory premises and was approaching the company gate, he was attacked by Mr Ramesh along with other seven to eight committee members and assaulted him.

It was seen by the security officer and he called the chairman and one of the directors from the office. Meanwhile, the attackers ran away from that place. Along with the help of chairman and the director, Mr Jadhav was treated in the hospital in Vashi and along with the doctor's report, a complaint was lodged by Mr Jadhav with Turbhe Police Station. All the accused were arrested by police and were given custody for three days thereafter. When Mr Ramesh was relieved from police custody, he approached Dr Sawant's union located at Ghatkopar station.

The union was known as 'Mazdoor Congress of Engineering workers'. When he met Dr Sawant, he requested him for representation on behalf of the workers of 'Dishends Ltd'. Dr Sawant advised him to enrol all the workers of the company as members of his union and, after collection of membership fees, to stop the work of the company and then to approach him for further action to be taken by the union. At the same time, he discussed with Mr Ramesh the details of general demands pending before management.

After a period of two days, Mr Ramesh brought a letter from Dr Sawant along with the same demands which they had put before the management through S.R. Kanitkar union and in the letter itself, it was demanded to settle these demands within eight days from the receipt of the demand letter of the union or otherwise workers would take the law into their hands and responsibility of the consequences would remain with the management.

After receiving this letter, the management decided to take disciplinary action against Mr Ramesh for assaulting the personnel manager and accordingly, on 15 January 1980, Mr Ramesh and other eight committee members were suspended pending an enquiry. The letter was issued to him at the company's gate by the security officer.

The company's gate was opened on 16th as usual and some of the workmen tried to enter the factory for their regular work, who were obstructed by Mr Ramesh and other committee members and they were not allowed to go inside the factory. Somehow staff members and the management employees went inside the factory premises and some of the sincere and faithful workmen also by force went inside the factories who were in the first shift. Near about 35 casual workers were also not allowed to go inside the factory premises for work.

Mr Ramesh gathered the other workers including casual workers and informed them that they had brought in Dr Sawant's union and he has instructed to stop the total work of the company and further steps would be taken by the union related to general demands. Further, it was observed by the management that most of the skilled and sincere workers wanted to cooperate with the management and not to accept membership of the union of Dr Sawant, because of the threats and the pressure from local leaders they had signed as members of Dr Sawant's union.

After getting feedback from the majority of the management staff and workmen, charge sheets were issued to Mr Ramesh and eight committee members and they were called for a domestic enquiry as per the rules. The charge sheets were related with violence inside the factory premises, assaulting management people and declaring illegal strike etc. And the enquiries arranged outside the factory premises to conduct it peacefully.

The situation in the factory was that faithful workers were frightened because of the threat given by the union and committee members. Majority of the workers who were willing to continue the production demanded for police protection for which management also agreed.

After looking at the gravity of the situation, at of the factory, ACP Thane, Mr Prakash Pawar took the initiative and visited the factory and promised the management and workmen who were present in the factory to provide police protection in and outside the factory premises, and to give protection while travelling in the bus from Mumbai to factory and back.

The company was working for further two months with police protection and moral support was given to the workmen and staff members by the management and police authorities. Meanwhile, a complaint was lodged by the management in the labour court of Thane for declaration of the same strike as illegal and no wages for striking days. The strike was declared illegal by the labour court, union and workmen were advised to restore the situation and join the duties unconditionally.

Meanwhile, after a period of two to three months, all the enquiries were completed by the management ex parte. And the decision taken by the management was the dismissal of Mr Ramesh along with eight committee members based on findings of the enquiry officer. The management of the company removed all the 35 casual workers also who did not report for their duties for more than three months. This information went to all the workmen of the company and nearby villages, which was shocking news in that local area.

Meanwhile, a local leader of Shivsena, Mr Kishor Salvi met Mr S.K. Jadhav and told him that majority of the workmen had requested him to protect their services and lives from Dr Sawant and local committee members who were dismissed from the services of the company; hence he wanted to represent the workmen and to cooperate with the management to run the company smoothly because it was a question of bread and butter of the local workmen as well as the survival of the company.

He also met the chairman of the company, Mr Mohanlal Yadav and promised him accordingly. Thereafter he formed a committee of new 11 unit committee members and sent an introduction letter to the company in the name of 'Shramik Sena union'. After the entry of 'Shramik Sena', Dr Sawant's members were troubling the faithful workmen and the management staff members.

The management, on request of Mr Kishor Salvi, recruited 35 new casual workers based on 'sons of soil' policy. Later it was informed to the government labour department. And the company also got sympathy from the Government of Maharashtra. Shramik Sena meanwhile made an application in industrial court of Thane for its recognition under MRTU and PULP Act 1971.

Application of Dr Sawant's union was pending before the labour court and industrial court related to illegal removal of Mr Ramesh and others including casual workers, were dismissed in due course. After a period of one year or so 'Shramik Sena' of Mr Kishor Salvi received a certificate of recognition in 'Dishends Ltd' and then the settlement took place by acceptance of 20 demands out of 25 original demands.

Case Questions

1. What were the reasons for industrial unrest in the company?

2. Was the dismissal of Trade Union leader and the committee members justified?

3. What is your response to the removal of 35 casual workers?

4. What is the legal position regarding casual workers in recognition of Trade Unions?

6

The Tiny Owl

A Case Study on the IR Issues at Start-ups

Learning Objectives

The start-up culture, while providing employment opportunities, is equally credited with creation of job crises for people who just got the string for their survival through employment with no guarantee of job security and long-term careers.

This is talking an alarming shape even with major start-ups changing hands as frequently as required to accumulate wealth through valuations and sale of assets to another venturist who may not guarantee any continuation of service and service terms to erstwhile employees before asset acquisition and as of now, there are no labour laws to intervene such situations of short-lived life cycle of ownerships of start-ups living the employees to fend for themselves each time the organization undergoes ownership change.

This situation has given rise to false employability assurances to the youth who are snatched of their career objectives even before they start planning for a career. While traditional industries are undergoing metamorphosis through technology changes imposed by AI and quite often resulting in reducing employment through downsizing exercises undertaken by these large companies, the plight of employees in uncertain start-ups is a cry in the wilderness.

Synopsis

The start-ups are mushrooming all across India even supported by the government policy and regulatory guideline as favourable to the

Indian Business Case Studies. Srilatha Palekar, Arun Pardhi and Sunanda Jindal, Oxford University Press. © ASM Group of Institutes, Pune, India 2022. DOI: 10.1093/oso/9780192869449.003.0006

promoters. But unfortunately, employment opportunities at the start-ups are like mutual fund investments are subject to unemployment risks since the start-ups, in general, are not meant to provide assurance of employee tenures since they are ever dynamic and wish to change their business models as often as required to keep the promoters investments providing best of revaluation results such that when an opportunity is apt, they can liquidate their stake to make money on revalued assets and dispose their engagement in the start-up.

Hence if someone is seeking a long-term career objective as an employee in a start-up perhaps it is a risky proposition.

Case Details of 'Tiny Owl' (A Start-up)

'When we decided to restructure our team, all the founding members made up their minds that we would individually go and break the news. Yes we could have sent managers to do it on our behalf but we took a more humanitarian approach to the problem. In retrospect I think we could have timed the announcement; better.

The festive time got people more upset than we expected. My personal experience says one only needs to be patient, that's the key. Yes the reactions of few employees are more emotional than we expected. We are doing the best in our capacity to help them pursue further opportunities. We are working day and night with our internal teams and investors to ensure that each and every employee of ours finds another job'. Tanuj Khandelwal, Co-founder of Tiny Owl (ET News Paper).

Tiny Owl is a private start-up company founded in 2014, headquartered in Mumbai, Maharashtra. Tiny Owl is a Mumbai-based food delivery company that essentially has two segments one deals with food ordering mobile app and other segment is Tiny Owl homemade.

The earlier one deals with a chain of leading local restaurants, i.e. customers will order food through the app and will get home delivery. The later segment deals with ordering food with a local chef. This is nothing but food tech space, was a genesis of Harsh Vardhan Mandad, taking another four friends to act as co-founder those are Gourav Chowdhary, Saurabh Goyal, Tanuj Khandelwal, and Shikhar Paliwal.

Mumbai-based food ordering start-up kick-started with $1 million in the juvenile stage by Sequoia Capital in August 2014 itself. In December 2014, another $3 million was raised from Sequoia and Nexus Venture Partners.

This pumping of another additional capital assisted the generation of food delivery system to 50 more cities in India. Preceding to it, in the month of February 2015, Tiny Owl raised capital to Rs. 100 crores in Series B funding. Within another six months, the investors like Sequoia Capital and Matrix Partners raised Rs. 50 crores.

In summary, we can say that Tiny Owl raised a total of $20 million in three rounds of funding. The company made a tie-up with over 4,000 restaurants across Mumbai, Pune, Gurgaon, Hyderabad, and Bengaluru. So, the reader can now digest the level of the tininess of Tiny Owl consisting of $1 million as expected revenues, daily 5,000 orders managed by 425 employees and the team of co-founders as support.

The Downward Spiral (Flow) of Tiny Owl

Private investors respond only to confident expectations of future security and growth. Such confidence will only be built up when those doing the investing recognize that the errors of the past have been corrected.

Once, an experienced CEO wrote in his blog about Tiny Owl 'Some difficult step towards the big dream' indicating their move of shutting shops in Delhi, Hyderabad, Pune, and Chennai, which in a way meant letting go off more employees. According to an ex-employee, 'this move was abrupt and disappointing' (ET News Paper).

Already two to three months ago, around July 2014 the start-up allegedly let go almost 300 employees stating cost-cutting as a reason. Employees were given a month's salary as a severance package a company would help them to find the job.

The Analysis

A successful employee engagement strategy helps to create a community at the workplace and not just the workforce. When the employees are effectively and positively engaged with their organization, they form an emotional connection with the company. This influences their attitude towards both their colleagues and the company's clients and improves customer satisfaction and service levels.

Needless to say, at Tiny Owl, the founders could have handled the whole separation process in a better manner. While they do agree that the employees did go overboard by holding a co-founder as a hostage for over 36 hours, at the same time, thinking is that this person shouldn't have gone to Pune in the first place. 'He was never in direct touch with employees so obviously making them understand the whole situation was a tough task for him, but at the same time holding him as a hostage and calling politicians and goons to put pressure on a 24-year-old co-founder was not ethical either', a former employee expressed.

This does not mean the safety of the other co-founders and same time, Shikhar Paliwal was taken hostage in Hyderabad. In another incident, Saurabh Goyal was taken hostage in Delhi. The reason for this task was the resentment against the company's refusal to pay salaries for the work done period.

On the other side of the coin, the management had a different story to tell, 'We have accounts to prove that all the salaries have been paid. Until we get a written confirmation from them that no physical harm will be caused to any of us, we are not going to clear the dues', a company source added (ET News Paper).

Eventually, all the co-founders were released after negotiating with the employees that all their settlements as per the employment terms will be settled, according to which the employees will be given a month's salary along with a month's notice period after they put up their papers.

However, agitated employees demanded a two-month salary along with a two-month notice period and the refusal from the management's side to fulfil this demand triggered the whole revolt.

Nevertheless, those who had resigned and agreed to abide by the contractual terms got their settlements cleared and those who demanded in excess of the employment terms will have to wait for a decision on it.

Though some of the employees couldn't stop raging about the company and management, another set of employees feels that hiring and firing should be considered as part and parcel of working in the start-up world. 'We all are aware of the risks associated with working in a startup.

I never had a problem with the company or the management, though the whole process of laying off was too fast and abrupt but anyway there are mistakes happening at both the ends', adds another former employee.

Albinder Dhindsa, CEO and co-founder of Grofers, comments, 'Startups fire employees all the time and people are ready to work with these companies with the mindset that this will be risky and in no way is a stable job. And most companies have given disclaimers also.

And because there is a general slowdown in the market and there is no alternative job opportunity, because of which people are getting a little sensitive about getting fired. Earlier, when people were laid off, they would get a job at some other company easily'.

So, on the basis of the above opinions and thought process going to held in media, one can definitely conclude that there should be a particular situation in which these employees are carefully protected and the utmost care should be taken to hire according to skillset required by the company and the situation of sudden disengagement be almost avoided.

Case Questions

1. What is your opinion about the company's action against employees?

2. On the basis of the recent economic scenario, what are possible ways to implement employee engagement practices in start-ups?

3. What are the ways through which existing employees can be laid off but still be retained in the company?

7

Bosch Is the Boss

A Case Study IR Issues

Learning Objectives

One of the series editors of these Case Volumes, Prof J.A. Kulkarni, has been a witness to a real-life situation at Bosch Group of organizations in India at MICO Bosch during 1969–1973. In fact, the situation of frequent IR and ER issues at this multinational German auto ancillary company does not seem to have changed much during the past five decades.

Earlier years, Bosch Group used to have frequent IR skirmishes basically on account of not so well-educated workmen and their leaders and most of the clashes used to be mostly on account of over-stressed work environment and a ruthless management culture of achieving targets before any employee claims approach.

While there was adequate employment security in Bosch Group from the beginning as also above average wage and financial incentives, the workmen always felt that they were terrorized by peer pressures of rigorous work hours without much of humane ambience at the workplace. In fact, the victims of workers' rage used to be mostly the supervisory staff who were sandwiched between demanding bosses and the revolting workforce at the prick of a small pin.

In spite of technological updation of operational processes and needed upgradation of technical skills at operative levels, the culture of increased peer pressure seems to have also increased with time and major expansion and diversification of products and processes.

This case study is of great interest and content as applicable to present-day major manufacturing industries wherein the organization's work

Indian Business Case Studies. Srilatha Palekar, Arun Pardhi and Sunanda Jindal, Oxford University Press. © ASM Group of Institutes, Pune, India 2022. DOI: 10.1093/oso/9780192869449.003.0007

culture is very sensitive to peer behaviour and work pressures even though the wages and benefits are one of the highest in the industry.

Synopsis

A case is about the industrial relation issues in Bosch with different plants in India. It has gone through legal proceedings, tremendous pressure from political bodies, employees are against the management. At the end, the industrial issue was handled well by Bosch and made a profit despite the adverse business scenario.

Bosch manufactures various products as diverse as diesel and gasoline fuel injection systems, automotive aftermarket products, auto electricals, special purpose machines, packaging machines, electric power tools, and security systems.

Bosch Auto Parts India

Auto components major, Bosch said it will lift lockout order at its Jaipur plant, which it had issued earlier due to the ongoing worker unrest in the facility. 'A conciliation meeting was held on April 13, 2015 between the management and labour union supported by the Labour Secretary, wherein it was agreed that the union will not indulge in a "go-slow" action and call off their hunger strike immediately and the company will lift the lockout with effect from first shift of April 15, 2015', Bosch Ltd. said in a filing to the BSE. The labour secretary has directed both parties to continue discussions for the long-term wage settlement, it added (MINT News Paper).

Bosch to Suspend Production at Bengaluru, Bidadi Plants for Two Days

Bosch had announced plans to suspend all production activity at its Jaipur plant for eight days from 26 December 2015 in order to adjust to the market demand. There is no financial impact on account of the proposed suspension of operations, Bosch said in a regulatory filing. Global auto parts major Bosch plans to suspend all production activity at its Bengaluru and Bidadi plants for two days from 30 December in order to adjust to the market demand. 'With a view to adjust production to meet the demand for products and to avoid unnecessary build up of inventory, it is proposed to suspend all manufacturing operations at the company's Bengaluru and Bidadi plants on 30 December and 31 December', Bosch said in a regulatory filing (MINT News Paper).

There is no financial impact on account of the proposed suspension of operations, it added. The company has already announced plans to suspend all production activity at its Jaipur plant for eight days from 26 December in order to adjust to the market demand. Bosch Group chairman of the board of management Volkmar Denner had stated that repeated incidents of labour unrest could hurt investments in India. Bosch shares ended at Rs.18,562 on BSE, up 0.79% from the previous close.

Bosch Q3 Net Doubles to Rs. 221 Crores as on February 2016

Net sales during the period under review rose by 13.27 per cent to Rs 2,697.89 crores as against Rs 2,381.64 crores in the same period a year ago. Auto component maker Bosch today said its standalone net profit has doubled to Rs 220.77 crores in the quarter ended 31 December. The company had posted a net profit of Rs 110.87 crores in the same period last fiscal, Bosch said in a BSE filing. Net sales during the period under review rose by 13.27 per cent to Rs 2,697.89 crores as against Rs 2,381.64 crores in the same period a year ago.

Revenue from the automotive products stood at Rs 2,311.33 crores compared with Rs 2,064.99 crore, the company said, adding revenue from other business was at Rs 425.58 crores as against Rs 336.03 crores. Bosch said its board has also approved the in-principle transfer of the starter motors and generators business under the automotive products segment to a wholly-owned arm, Robert Bosch Starter Motors Generators Holding GmbH, which is being incorporated for a lump sum consideration of Rs 486.2 crores. Bosch Ltd. shares were trading 5.29 per cent lower at Rs 16,080.00 on BSE during the pre-close session.

About Bosch

The Bosch Group is a leading global supplier of technology and services. It employs roughly 375,000 associates worldwide (as of 31 December 2015). According to preliminary figures, the company generated sales of more than 70 billion euros in 2015. Its operations are divided into four business sectors: mobility solutions, industrial technology, consumer goods, and energy and building technology. The Bosch Group comprises Robert Bosch GmbH and its roughly 440 subsidiaries and regional companies in some 60 countries. If its sales and service partners are included, then Bosch is represented in roughly 150 countries. This worldwide development, manufacturing, and sales network are the foundation for further growth. In 2015, Bosch applied for some 5,400 patents worldwide. The Bosch Group's strategic objective is to deliver innovations for a connected life. Bosch improves the quality of life worldwide with products and services that are innovative and spark enthusiasm. In short, Bosch creates technology that is 'Invented for life'.

The company was set up in Stuttgart in 1886 by Robert Bosch (1861–1942) as 'Workshop for Precision Mechanics and Electrical Engineering'. The special ownership structure of Robert Bosch GmbH guarantees the entrepreneurial freedom of the Bosch Group, making it possible for the company to plan over the long term and to undertake significant up-front investments in the safeguarding of its future.

Ninety-two per cent of the share capital of Robert Bosch GmbH is held by Robert Bosch Stiftung GmbH, a charitable foundation. The majority of voting rights are held by Robert Bosch Industrietreuhand KG, an industrial trust. The entrepreneurial ownership functions are carried out by the trust. The remaining shares are held by the Bosch family and by Robert Bosch GmbH.

Bosch Company History

1. 1886–1900: The Workshop for Precision Mechanics and Electrical Engineering
2. 1901–1923: Becoming a global automotive supplier West Germany

3. 1924–1945: From automotive supplier to diversified group West Germany
4. 1946–1959: Rebuilding and the economic miracle
5. 1960–1989: Founding of the divisions and breakthrough in electronics
6. 1990–2015: Solutions to the challenges of globalization—a determined leader.

About Bosch in India

In India, Bosch is a leading supplier of technology and services in the areas of mobility solutions, industrial technology, consumer goods, and energy and building technology. Additionally, Bosch has in India the largest development centre outside Germany, for end-to-end engineering and technology solutions. The Bosch Group operates in India through nine companies, viz, Bosch Ltd., Bosch Chassis Systems India Ltd., Bosch Rexroth India Ltd., Robert Bosch Engineering and Business Solutions Pvt. Ltd., Bosch Automotive Electronics India Pvt. Ltd., Bosch Electrical Drives India Pvt. Ltd., BSH Home Appliances Pvt. Ltd., ETAS Automotive India Pvt. Ltd., and Robert Bosch Automotive Steering India Pvt. Ltd.

In India, Bosch set up its manufacturing operation in 1953, which has grown over the years to include 14 manufacturing sites and seven development and application centres. Bosch Group in India employs over 29,000 associates and generated consolidated revenue of about Rs. 15,250 crores*. The Group in India has close to 12,000 research and development associates and has filed for around 150 patents in 2014. In India, Bosch Ltd. is the flagship company of the Bosch Group. It earned revenue of over Rs. 9,570 crores in 2014.

Employees of Bosch Bangalore Plant Go on Strike in March 2013

The employee union of Bosch Ltd., MICO (Bosch's Indian subsidiary was earlier known as Motor Industries Company Ltd.) Employee's Association (MEA), has begun a 'tool down' strike at the Bosch Bangalore plant.

The company has called it illegal. The strike is the result of the suspension of a workman at the plant.

The company, which makes automotive components and systems, has had a history of union unrest with the latest strike being the second such in the last 18 months.

A statement issued by Bosch read, 'It was observed that some associates deployed in a new production line were unwilling to meet basic production requirements in accordance with the standards of industrial engineering'.

'Over the past three months, the workmen adopted a "go-slow" approach producing significantly lower than earlier attained levels. After much deliberation, disciplinary action resulting in suspension of one of the identified workmen was taken' (MINT News Paper). The company added that it was in dialogue with the MEA and the labour commissioner to resolve the strike.

In October 2011, MEA had launched a similar 'tool down' strike to protest the company's decision to outsource certain non-core manufacturing and support processes from its Bangalore plant in a bid to reduce costs and competitively price its products.

In 2010 too, there was a 'tool down' strike that led to Bosch declaring a complete lockdown after the union employees physically intimidated and threatened managers of the plant. The manufacturing sector, in particular the auto sector, has been witnessing major strikes around the country.

Bosch Bengaluru plant 'tool down' strike was called off in March 2013. The employee union of Bosch Limited–MEA (MICO Employee's Association) has called off the strike post discussion with the Bosch Management on 9 March 2013. The management and the union meeting concluded with a quick resolution on the issues, supported by the intervention of Additional Labour Commissioner.

An agreement was reached on the working model for the new production line as per well-established industrial engineering standards. Based on this, the suspension of one employee has been withdrawn; however, the enquiry on the employee will still continue. The workmen have resumed work at the factory premises starting from the night shift of 9 March 2013.

A quick resolution to the issues has been reached, however, practices like 'go-slow' and the illegal tool down strike, affecting the employees and the company, must be avoided. Bosch management stresses that in accordance with its reputation as a fair employer, all decisions pertaining to business shall be in favour of the organization and its employees. Bosch will continue to act fairly yet firmly in all such situations.

Bosch Strike: Talks with Management on 17 September 2014 to Resolve Issues

The first round of talks with the management would be held 18 September 2014 to resolve issues at German auto component major Bosch Ltd.'s Adugodi plant, where a strike by workers entered the second day today, a union official said (MINT News Paper).

'We will be holding a bilateral talks with the management as per the direction of Additional Labour Commissioner Narasimhamurthy to solve issues pending for the past 22 months, MICO Employees Association President S Prasanna Kumar told PTI here.

The workers had gone on 'tool down' strike. After the bilateral meeting, a tripartite meeting, involving the union, the company management and the Additional Labour Commissioner, will be held on 20 September, he said.

The workers had gone on an indefinite strike claiming that the management planned to cut down some medical benefits and demanded productivity 'which cannot logically happen to the level of their expectation'. While the company in a filing to the BSE described the demands of the workers as 'unreasonable' and the strike is illegal. The company has 2,575 permanent workers, 700 temporary workers, and 1,000 contract workers, Kumar said. The management has also started issuing transfer orders to employees to shift to Bidadi plant near Bangalore without even discussing facilities like transport, he said.

The company's Bangalore plant has a history of workers' unrest, and the plant was shut down temporarily following a strike in September 2011.

Striking Bosch Workers in India Defy State Government Ban in October 2014

Striking Bosch workers at the Adugodi plant in Bangalore, southern India, are continuing a five-week strike for higher wages and better conditions, defying the outlawing of their strike by the Karnataka state government.

They are demanding a wage rise of at least 20 percent, a refund of wage cuts imposed on workers for earlier strikes, an end to harassment, and the reinstatement of victimized workers. They are also fighting for permanency for temporary workers with more than 240 days' service, a halt to a Valid Time (VT) study, which aims to increase production targets, and the reversal of health scheme cuts.

In a blatant bid to break the strike on behalf of Bosch, the Congress Party state government banned it on 10 October, invoking the 1947 Industrial Disputes Act. The company immediately demanded that workers end the strike, branding it 'illegal'. As a punitive measure, the company announced an eight-hour pay cut for every hour of striking.

On 14 October, Karnataka police arrested around 150 strikers when a thousand gathered in front of Chief Minister Siddaramaiah's residence to protest the government's ban. They were later released on bail.

German-based Bosch is one of the biggest automobile spare parts manufacturers in India. It has another plant in Bangalore—at Nagnathpura, on the state capital's outskirts—one at Nasik in Maharashtra, western India, and one at Jaipur in Rajasthan, northern India. Bosch India, a major supplier to companies like Toyota and Maruti Suzuki, recorded a net profit of Rs 8.85 billion ($US308 million) in 2013 and Rs 6.33 billion in the first two quarters of this year.

Bosch's Adugodi plant has 2,300 permanent workers, 370 temporary workers, and 1,000 contract workers. On average, permanent workers are paid just Rs 40,000 ($649.3) a month. New entrant workers and temporary workers are paid about half that. Some young workers, employed as 'job trainees', get only Rs 13,000 per month, can be forced to work on all three shifts, and can be fired at any moment.

The company maintains this multi-tier workforce to divide workers and extract higher profits. But permanent, temporary, and contract workers have joined the strike, cutting across the management's attempt to split them.

Workers have been denied a salary increment since it was due in January 2013. They rejected a management offer of Rs 5,500 monthly rise, which does not cover the rising cost of living, and demanded an increase of Rs 8,500.

When the Workers Social Welfare Society (WSWS) interviewed strikers, one explained that the VT study aims to increase production targets to unreachable levels and thus abolish current incentives paid to workers. The management even removed seating arrangements for production workers, forcing them to stand, compromising their health.

Another striker denounced new limits imposed by the management on the medical reimbursement scheme. 'Every worker pays a monthly premium of 909 rupees for the medical reimbursement', he explained. 'Now the compensation for major illness is limited at 150,000 rupees and compensation for serious illnesses like cancer is limited at 500,000 rupees' (MINT News Paper).

While the Bosch strikers are determined to fight, their union, the MEA, only reluctantly called the strike in the face of the mounting anger of workers. The union leaders have led workers on several marches to make appeals to the same government that has banned their strike.

In response to the 14 October arrests of strikers, MEA president Prasanna Kumar said: 'We went there to peacefully make our submissions to the chief minister and make him understand that the government's decision is in favour of management'. Even after the ban, the union is trying to promote illusions that the government can be convinced to support the strikers.

The MEA is working to isolate the strikers. It has not called on workers at the nearby Nagnathpura plant to join the strike, let alone other Bosch workers. It has made no appeal to workers in other industries. This flows from the politics of the MEA leaders.

President Kumar is associated with the Centre for Indian Trade Unions (CITU), affiliated to Stalinist Communist Party of India (Marxist) or CPM. The general secretary, Amarjeet Bhatia, who claims to be 'independent', is affiliated to the Industry All Global Union (IAGU). Other office bearers are associated with the Indian Trade Union Congress (INTUC), the union wing of Congress, which holds office in Karnataka and led the previous national government for 10 years.

As for the IAGU, like all international trade unions, it functions on behalf of major corporations to suppress industrial action. In a 5 October letter to the IAGU, MEA general secretary Bhatia said he had urged Bosch 'to urgently conduct an audit at Bosch Adugodi plant in connection with human rights violations, unfair labour practices, un-ergonomic work practices, inhuman working environment, compression work culture and other malpractices' (MINT News Paper). Bhatia asked an opportunity for the MEA to meet with a member of Bosch's board.

Far from there being any differences between Bosch's Indian branch and its parent company in Germany, the appalling working conditions in Adugodi plant are driven directly by the profit interests of the German-based company.

More than 2,575 workers at the plant in Adugodi in the city went on strike on 16 September at the end of the legally stipulated notice period, demanding a new wage agreement to replace the one that lapsed in December 2012.

Although the gap between what the company was willing to give the workers and what the workers were willing to settle for appeared to be narrow, the difference was 'a matter of principle', said S. Prasanna Kumar, MICO Employees Association. The two main unresolved issues pertaining to medical benefits and the manner in which labour productivity is calculated. Prasanna Kumar said a solution to the question of medical benefits seemed imminent, but the company's position on labour productivity—and hence workers' wages—was characterized by 'ambiguity'.

Prasanna Kumar, also a general secretary of CITU, said labour productivity should be based on a scientific study of time and motion of man and machine on the shop floor. He also said that although the existing productivity levels at the Adugodi plant were higher than those based on scientific norms, the company was unwilling to accept this and reward the workers. 'The company's stand is not based on any scientific principle, nor does it comply with any standardized productivity measure', he claimed. He added that although the difference between the two sides, in financial terms, appeared to be only a few thousand rupees, the company's 'unwillingness to protect the workers' existing wages (achieved through higher productivity) reflects a stubborn and intransigent position that has no basis in any scientific method'.

Although the Karnataka Labour Department initiated talks on 18 September, it failed to break the deadlock. The company appealed for an 'adjudication process', implying that the dispute be resolved through a judicial process, which the union rejected. The union pointed out that allowing an already delayed wage settlement to pass through such a tortuous process was not only illogical but bad in law.

Ironically, the prolonged slowdown in the Indian automotive industry, which resulted in the pile-up of inventory levels, may be favourable to Bosch as it engages in a tussle with its workforce. But, clearly, recurring disputes with its workforce do not augur well for a company that likes to project itself as an 'ideal' employer.

Although the dispute veered towards a settlement in the second week of the strike, following the narrowing of the gap between the two sides, the union leadership is clear in its understanding that the question of the imbalance between the increase in productivity that workers deliver and the wages they earn remains a 'fundamentally unresolved question'. 'But that is a longer and wider battle, which we will continue to fight', said Prasanna Kumar. **The 62-day ongoing strike has led to an estimated loss of around 2% of overall turnover registered during the period of the agitation.**

Multinational engineering firm Bosch isn't really unfamiliar with labour trouble when it comes to its operations in India. But the ongoing 62-day strike at its biggest plant in the country, in Bangalore, is turning out to be one of the most protracted standoffs between the company and its workers in recent years.

The labour-related woes faced by the German company in Bangalore come in the midst of an ambitious 'Make in India' campaign, which aims to put Indian manufacturing on the global map. Bosch's experience of dealing with its Indian workforce may put off potential global investors. It prompted the company's global chairman Volkmar Denner to comment, during his recent India visit, that repeated labour trouble could make Indian manufacturing uncompetitive.

Unlike the two relatively shorter 'tool-down' strikes that Bosch's Bangalore plant witnessed in 2013, the current one has been prohibited by the Karnataka government after conciliatory talks mediated by the state's labour department failed about a month ago. The Bosch workers' union, called MEA, challenged that order in the Karnataka High Court which gave the management and the union a chance to resolve the issue bilaterally. As no settlement was reached, the court will now take up the matter for hearing.

So far, the strike has led to an estimated loss of around 2 per cent of overall turnover registered during the period of the agitation that started on 16 September. But it hasn't hurt the company's July–September quarter earnings in which Bosch posted a net profit of Rs 306.7 crores, a year-on-year increase of 30.8%. This was largely helped by an increase in non-operating income from the sale of some marketable securities. 'It (strike) will have some minor effect in the performance in the subsequent quarter. We are keen to resolve the issues with our union as we look forward to sustaining our growth and competitiveness in the market', said Steffen Berns, managing director, Bosch Ltd.

Bosch Group in India generated sales of Rs 13,200 crores in the year ended 31 December 2013. Bosch Ltd., the flagship company of the group in India, posted a profit after tax of Rs 885 crores, on net sales of Rs 8,641 crores in 2013. India is also home to Bosch's largest R&D centre outside Germany with around 10,500 engineers. According to Berns, the number of patents filed from the centre grew more than tenfold to 220 patents last year from around 20 registered innovations in 2008.

The labour trouble at Bosch's Bangalore plant, formerly known as Motor Industries Co, which makes diesel pumps and common rail systems for vehicles, comes at a time when the auto industry has been going through a rough patch and may not have as adverse an impact on the firm as it could have otherwise. Declining auto sales has taken a toll on the auto ancillary sector as well. In fiscal 2014, the turnover of India's auto component industry declined 2 per cent to Rs 2,11,765 crores ($35.13 billion). Several manufacturers including Bosch had to declare no-production days at their plants to prevent inventory pile-up.

Conclusions

Bosch is facing a lot of employee-related problems, which ultimately turn into strike and lockout situations. It follows the legal proceedings but at the end, the company stands strongly. They deal with such situations strategically. The ultimate goal of every organization is profit which is ultimately achieved by the company. They handle the situation and make way for profit. The company really works as a BOSS in different situations.

Case Questions

1. Explain the different strategies used by the company to deal with strike and lockout situations.

2. How can the company earn a profit despite all industrial relation issues?

3. What strategies are used by employees union to put forth their demands?

8

Enterprise and Ethics

The Two Pillars of an Empire: A Case Study on India's One of the Oldest Family-Managed Group of Companies

Learning Objectives

India's industrial legacy is full of examples of home-grown family-managed business groups known for their philanthropy and high core value-based organizational vision mission and operating culture.

Till today many of these organizations have grown huge in their business volumes not only in terms of business but also as organizations as role models of high placed organizational ethical core values and emphasis on corporate social responsibility as practiced.

The house of Godrej is one such group which every Indian is proud about their business ethics and never say die approach in adherence to human values as an integral part of their organizational culture. Perhaps the strength of such core values is that their businesses spread across different segments are fair and firm in their dealing with internal and external stakeholders. Money and business profits have never been the business drivers as against belief in their entrepreneurial capabilities and investing in sound business opportunities are in focus most of the times.

There are other Indian business groups such as the Tatas, Birlas, Infosys, Bajaj, and Mahindra with impeccable business ethics and more than fulfilling their social responsibilities over decades of successful entrepreneurial initiatives.

This case study is on Godrej, the people from safety locks, manufacturing precision machinery to senior living apartments explaining a few of their business beliefs and practices.

Indian Business Case Studies. Srilatha Palekar, Arun Pardhi and Sunanda Jindal, Oxford University Press. © ASM Group of Institutes, Pune, India 2022. DOI: 10.1093/oso/9780192869449.003.0008

Synopsis

How the Godrej Group channelled the swadeshi spirit at home, and then went global in 1989, when the vestiges of the license Raj era still wove reams of red tape around Indian businesses, a management trainee at Godrej GE Appliances' Faridabad office faced a dilemma. An excise tax collector wanted a Diwali 'gift' delivered at his residence. 'Or else ... '

After discussions with his seniors, the trainee turned up at the official's house the next day with a gift-wrapped box. At the visitor's insistence, the official unwrapped it, to find a pack of Godrej soaps in various fragrances. The unspoken but clear message: 'The Godrej group is committed to ethical business. Don't expect anything else from us'. The anecdote, narrated by Ranganatha Thota, the management trainee at that time, sums up an idea that Gurcharan Das, former CEO of Procter and Gamble India, has articulated: while India secured political independence in 1947, it got economic independence only with the 1991 reforms.

In many ways, the business history of the Godrej Group, which dates back to 1897, mirrors the Independence movement. The group's founder Ardeshir Godrej, as the Godrej Rhyme narrates and as BK Karanjia chronicles in his two-volume book *Godrej: A Hundred Years 1897–1997*, left India for Africa in 1889 to practise law. But unwilling to commit perjury to advance his career, he returned home, where the freedom movement was gathering pace, with the birth of the Indian National Congress in 1885.

Case Details

Upon returning to India, Ardeshir became an early proponent of the swadeshi idea of economic self-reliance. An early venture to manufacture medical equipment failed owing to British protectionism, but the indefatigable entrepreneur cast his eye on lowly locks. The lock business was in the control of British and American manufacturers, but Ardeshir found a flaw in their products: their springs, used to work the levers, often gave way. Borrowing money to set up a shed in Lalbaug in Mumbai in 1897, he began making Anchor locks, which didn't have springs. They were well-received in the market. From that, he went on to manufacture safes, again exposing a chink in the foreign-made safes, which rendered them unreliable. He patented the door frame, double-plate doors, and lock-case, and sold his safes at half the price of foreign brands. So successful was this business that even the Queen, while on a tour of India in 1912, availed of the services of a Godrej safe.

Ardeshir Godrej, who had a renaissance spirit that was always looking for new realms to conquer, then began manufacturing soap with vegetable oil, out of consideration for Hindu sentiments that disfavoured the use of animal fat. His soaps soon secured celebrity endorsements from Rabindranath Tagore, Dr Annie Besant, and C Rajagopalachari. Despite the heavily skewed business landscape that protected British business interests, Godrej products held their own against multinationals. By the time he died in 1936, Ardeshir had expanded Godrej's businesses into new areas. That year, Godrej & Boyce and Godrej Soaps posted revenues of Rs 12 lakhs and Rs 6 lakhs, respectively.

Consolidation Phase

Ardeshir's younger brother Pirojsha, who succeeded him, focussed on consolidation rather than expansion into new areas. By Independence, the Group's revenues had grown five times to Rs 90 lakhs. In 1948, the company secured permission to construct its first manufacturing plant on a large parcel of land that Pirojsha had acquired in Vikhroli (in current-day Mumbai). What it manufactured first was not locks or safes, but secure ballot boxes for independent India's first elections in 1952.

To showcase Indian prowess in manufacturing—the original 'Make in India' campaign!—Godrej diversified into making typewriters in 1953. Only four of the 1,800 components were imported; even these were soon being made at home. At the Congress session at Avadi, in Madras, Jawaharlal Nehru stooped over a Godrej typewriter to tip-tap a few words, signalling India's early success in industrialization. Pirojsha then ventured into making refrigerators; in 1958, the first Indian fridge came with a Rs 1,885 tag. Pirojsha got his three sons on board: Sohrabji to look into the overall marketing of Godrej products, Burjorji to look after soaps, and Naval to look into typewriters, refrigerators, and hi-tech electronics.

Going Global

The 1960s were a decade of two wars, a drought, and rampant inflation. In 1963, in the midst of that crisis, Burjorji's son Adi Godrej took over the soaps business, which then had a turnover of Rs 2.43 crores. This was the decade when the Group gained a global footprint. After a couple of false starts, it secured a foothold in Malaysia and, later, Singapore. By the 1970s, exports to western Europe picked up. Pirojsha passed away in 1972; by then, the third generation of the Godrej family was in the saddle, with Naval's son Jamshyd heading the steel business, while Adi took Godrej soaps to new heights.

By 1975, the Group's exports touched Rs 22 crores. Inspired by Japanese processes, it introduced the Godrej Management System, to improve productivity and reduce inventories. The dawn of the 1980s was marked by fierce competition with Hindustan Lever in the soaps segment. 'We needed big ideas to take on the competition and for the first time a male protagonist was used to promote a soap brand', recalls advertising incharge Sam Balsara, who handled the Cinthol account. The campaign in 1985 featured Vinod Khanna on horseback and, later, Imran Khan. Both proved phenomenal hits.

Post-1991 Phase

When the gale force of economic reforms came sweeping in 1991, Godrej was poised for take-off. In the 25 years since, the Group has grown into a $4.5 billion (Rs 30,000 crores) conglomerate, with an impressive global footprint. These 25 years have also seen the Group experiment, unsuccessfully, with joint ventures with GE, P&G, Sara Lee, Pillsbury, and Hershey. And in 2008, when the global financial crisis dragged down economies, the Group, now into its fourth-generation leadership under Adi's daughter Tanya Dubash, underwent a rebranding exercise to extend the brand appeal to young customers. Looking ahead, the Group plans to stick to its growth target of '10x in 10 years', growing both organically and through acquisitions. Industry analysts feel the Group will deliver. 'They truly walk the talk', says Nilesh Shah, Managing Director, Kotak Mutual Fund.

It's been 119 years since Ardeshir, the low-profile Parsi gentleman, implanted the Godrej flag in the land that adopted his Guderz tribe (from which the family name derives) that fled from Iran. In this time, the Godrej Group has established itself not only as an entrepreneurial success but also as a business that runs on strong ethical foundations.

As Safe as Godrej

The Group's product portfolio ranges from soaps to safety devices to aerospace manufacturing.

When independent India's first general elections were to take place in 1951–1952, the government had to find a manufacturer for the ballot boxes. It zeroed in on Godrej & Boyce, which was by then already known for its high-quality locks and lockers. The company's factory in Vikhroli started operations in July 1951 and produced 15,000 ballot boxes a day to meet the order of 12 lakh boxes from 23 states. The cost per box: Rs 5.

'With external locks proving expensive, Nathalal Panchal, a workman at Godrej, devised a unique locking system. It could only be opened by breaking a pre-impressed insignia and manipulating the locking lever through the aperture covered by the insignia', explains Vrunda Pathare, chief archivist at Godrej. One of these ballot boxes adorns the conglomerate's archives in suburban Vikhroli.

Back in 1947, Godrej was not only offering security solutions. The Group had also started manufacturing cupboards and soaps. 'Soap production was a result of the vow to use swadeshi products in pre-independent India. Sir Ardeshir Godrej came out with a washing soap bar in 1918 and toilet soap in 1920', says Pathare. The first vegetable-oil soap was named 'No. 2' while No. 1 came in 1922. This soap continues to be popular in India even today.

The Godrej Group's history does not begin from the 20th century. It was in 1897 in a tiny shed in Mumbai's Lalbaugh area that Ardeshir Godrej came out with a high-security lock, branded as Anchor. This shed eventually became the shopfloor for churning out various products using metal sheets. Today, however, operations have shifted entirely to Vikhroli. Godrej was also called upon to provide safes for the Queen of England when she visited India in 1905. Today, Godrej Security Solutions caters not only to domestic clients but also exports to 45 countries. The Group's manufacturing extends even to aerospace components.

Generations of Godrej employees have grown up and followed in the footsteps of their parents and grandparents in the company. Javed Khan, Head of Operations at Hubble (the Group's collaborative workspace division), says his grandfather Sikander Khan worked for 35 years in the electricity department and his father Amir Khan spent close to four decades in the Group's manufacturing division.

'After studying in the UK, I joined Godrej in 2010. I have worked in other companies too, but I find the working conditions the best here', he says (TOI News Paper). The Group not only takes care of employees' housing, schooling, and medical needs but it also offers freedom to work and execute ideas, says Khan. 'There is a culture of promoting entrepreneurship within the organisation. My business idea has been sponsored by the group', he adds.

Somewhat similar is the story of Khushnuma Khambatta, associate general manager at Godrej Interio. Her father worked for over four decades in multiple roles from marketing to manufacturing. He retired in 2014, while Khushnuma had joined the Group in 2001. 'When I was a kid, my father bought home books on the group. I grew up seeing a company that had an Indian fabric and a global vision. It made me want to work for Godrej', she says.

After evolving from manufacturing to marketing, the Godrej group is now focused on design and innovation. It is this continuous reinvention of the Group that stands it in good stead to thrive in the coming centuries as well.

Case Questions

1. In spite of the breakneck competition in each industry and the mad rush for adopting the latest technology and global expansion plans, including major acquisitions, how is it possible that businesses like Godrej have been able to sustain and maintain extremely cordial IR situation as also voluntarily fulfilling major corporate responsibilities? How does the business manage its competitiveness in cost quality and schedule adherence?

2. What is the importance of an ethical approach in all the business processes which helps a company to thrive in spite of highly volatile and competitive forces in its marketplace?

3. How does Godrej manage diversity in a global ethical dilemma and generational gaps in business management attitudes and remains intact as a successful family-managed business?

9

Corporate Social Responsibility

The Amway Approach: A Case Study in CSR

Learning Objectives

Managing business growth through customer engagement is a novel business concept followed by Amway, one of the very popular business groups in India.

Amway is unique in effectively utilizing the age-old concept of live and let live wherein their first-line customer group gets engaged as sales outlets for business growth. However, Amway takes the full responsibility of attending to customer satisfaction needs.

Amway, by extending the basic business framework, has been serving its customers like a family member, constantly in touch with the periodical needs of its members. With this business philosophy, Amway has spread its business across the globe, initiating joint activities with UNICEF and many associations to help children to get timely help for their health and educational needs.

This case study tries to explain in its limited scope the way Amway has been able to serve the society and simultaneously manage its business objectives.

Synopsis

Responsibility (CSR Corporate Social) means businesses communities they and organizations working responsibly and contributing positively to the operations. It involves working with employees, their families, the local community, and society at large to improve their quality of life.

Indian Business Case Studies. Srilatha Palekar, Arun Pardhi and Sunanda Jindal, Oxford University Press. © ASM Group of Institutes, Pune, India 2022. DOI: 10.1093/oso/9780192869449.003.0009

Amway	UNICEF
is a global business.	is the United Nations Children's Fund
Amway is one of the world's largest direct sales companies.	UNICEF is the world's leading organisation working for children.
It has over 3 million Independent Business Owners (IBOs) Worldwide.	It is a global champion of children's rights.

Companies that operate in a socially responsible way strengthen their reputations. In business, reputation is everything. It determines the extent to which customers want to buy from you, partners are willing to work with you, and you're standing in the community.

The Company

Amway is one of the world's largest direct sales organizations with over 3 million independent business owners (IBOs) in over 80 markets and territories worldwide. It is a family-owned business with a strong emphasis on family values. Its IBOs are often couples. Many of these are raising families. They therefore have a strong bond with children. These families are more than happy to partner with Amway, who, as part of its corporate social responsibility (CSR) strategy, works with the United Nations Children's Fund (UNICEF).

As a family company, Amway is committed to playing a part in improving the lives of children in need across the globe. In this way, the company is able to show its commitment to the support of global causes.

Amway defines a global cause as 'a social issue affecting many people around the world engaged in a struggle or plight that warrants a charitable response'.

This case study shows how Amway is a business that does more than providing customers with good quality products. It shows the practical realities of Amway's global commitment and how it plays a key role in the communities in which it operates.

Growth and Responsibility

An understanding of how Amway operates as an organization gives a clearer picture of the contribution it can make to help children in need across the globe. Amway's vision is to help people live better lives. It does this every day by providing a low-cost, low-risk business opportunity based on selling quality products.

What Does Amway Do?

Amway distributes a range of branded products. These products are sold to IBOs worldwide. The IBOs are Amway's links with consumers and the communities in which they operate. The IBOs are self-employed and are highly motivated. They work within the guidelines of Amway's Rules of Conduct and Code of Ethics, which are about being honest and responsible in trading. IBOs sell to people that they know or meet. They can introduce others to the Amway business.

Typical products that IBOs sell include:

- personal care fragrances, body care
- skincare and cosmetics
- durables such as cookware and water treatment systems
- nutrition and wellness products such as food supplements, food, and drinks.

IBOs play a key part in helping Amway to deliver its Global Cause Programme.

Amway Programmes

In order to give many of the world's children a chance to live a better life, Amway launched the global One by One campaign for children in 2003. Amway encourages staff and IBOs to support its One by One campaign for children. The One by One programme:

- helps Amway to bring its vision to life
- declares what the company stands for
- builds trust and respect in Amway brands
- establishes CSR at a high level.

Since 2001, Amway Europe has been an official partner of UNICEF and has been able to contribute over 2 million Euros (about £1.4 million). The focus is on supporting the worldwide 'Immunization Plus' program.

This involves, for example, providing measles vaccines to children across the globe. The 'Plus' is about using the vehicle of immunization to deliver other life-saving services for children. It is about making health systems stronger and promoting activities that help communities and families to improve child-care practices. For example, the 'Plus' could include providing vitamin A supplements in countries where there is vitamin A deficiency.

The need is great. One out of ten children in Kenya does not live to see its fifth birthday, largely through Since 2001, Amway and its IBOs across Europe have been supporting UNICEF's child survival programme. preventable diseases like Malaria which is one of the biggest killer with 93 deaths per day. Only 58% of children under two are fully immunized as of date.

The work of the One by One programme is illustrated by a field trip undertaken by Amway IBOs to Kenya. The IBOs travelled to Kilifi in 2006 to meet children and to find out what the problems are in various communities. They act as champions spreading the message throughout their groups. In Kilifi, the focus is on trying to reach the most vulnerable children and pregnant mothers. The aim is to increase immunization from 40% to 70%. Other elements of the programme involve seeking to prevent the transmission of HIV/AIDS to infants. As the Amway organization grows and prospers, it is able, through CSR actions, to help communities to grow and prosper too.

Developing a strategy is an organizational plan. Implementing a strategy involves putting that plan into action. In other words, a strategy shows how a business will achieve its goals. The strategy thus enables an organization to turn its values into action. Values are what a company stands for. An important value for Amway is being a caring company. Amway believes in demonstrating this caring approach and this is why it has partnered with UNICEF.

All directors design strategies for the whole of an organization. Effective strategies involve discussion and communication with others. The views of IBOs are influential in creating strategies for Amway. Amway's strategies for CSR are cascaded through the organization, as shown later.

Amway's Global Cause strategy involves creating responsible plans that make a difference. However, the strategy is flexible. In shaping the strategy, research was carried out to find out which global causes IBOs support. The results showed that many favoured a cause that helped children. There was a clear fit between Amway's aims to help children and UNICEF's 'Immunization Plus' programme for children.

Objectives

From the outset, Amway set out some clear objectives for its strategy. These were to:

- build loyalty and pride among IBOs and employees
- enhance Amway's reputation as a caring organization
- make a real difference in human lives.

Child mortality is particularly high in developing countries because of infectious diseases. Many children could still be alive if they had been vaccinated. For under £12, a child can be vaccinated against these diseases and has a fighting chance to reach adulthood. UNICEF's world child 'Immunization Plus' programme is a fitting focus for the activities of Amway UK and its IBOs.

The UK initiative is part of a European-wide fundraising campaign for children. It recognizes the importance of building good working relationships with UNICEF in each market in order to launch fundraising programmes through Amway's IBOs and their customers. The objective is to raise 500,000 Euros (about £350,000) every year until 2010 across Amway Europe.

In 2005, Amway UK's partnership was deepened through becoming an official Corporate Partner of UNICEF UK. The corporate partnership is a closer longer-term relationship that benefits both partners. Working together, the two parties raise money for UNICEF.

Identifying Stakeholders

Amway's CSR strategy has been developed with the interests of all its stakeholders in mind.

Communicating the Strategy

Good, clear communication is essential in making sure that the CSR strategy relates directly to the company's business objectives. Communication also helps in putting the strategy into practice.

A number of communication media are used:

1. Face-to-face communication: Regular meetings take place between UNICEF, Amway, and its IBOs. Through meetings with UNICEF staff, Amway is able to discuss the vision and objectives. It then passes the message on by meeting with IBOs. In 2005, the two organizations arranged a joint briefing day for IBO Leaders. They were able to hear first-hand experiences from UNICEF staff about their roles and UNICEF's work as well as where the money goes.
2. Printed material: Amway produces a monthly magazine for all IBOs called Amagram.
3. Public relations materials are also important, particularly at launch events for the initiative (e.g. in Milton Keynes in 2006).

4. Email communication: Email is very important in the company; it plays a significant part in keeping IBOs up-to-date.
5. Online activities: There is a micro-site dedicated to the Amway UK/ UNICEF partnership on the UNICEF UK website.

Fund Raising

Amway Europe provides support for fundraising to the extent of 500,000 Euros (about £350,000) per year through selling items such as:

- greetings cards
- multi-cultural gifts and cards
- stationery and wrapping paper
- toys for children

However, Amway UK's support goes well beyond these activities. In addition, it involves staff fundraising events and raffles organized by the IBOs.

UNICEF attends IBO major events (usually supported by 1,000 or more IBOs) where requested. A UNICEF stand outlines the work with speakers, literature, and merchandise.

Conclusions

Amway is a family business with family values. Its IBOs are people who want to make a difference to the communities in which they operate and to the wider world community. This is CSR in action. The clue to Amway's success is the careful planning of its strategy and its involvement with many stakeholders in getting the strategy right. Of course, it is early days in the latest chapter of a strong relationship between Amway and UNICEF.

Evaluation is taking place to measure the success of the initiative in terms of meeting fundraising goals. Customer research is carried out to test customers' views on the relationship and to find out how aware the general public is about what Amway is doing in the field of CSR.

Case Questions

1. How does Amway manage its product development and market growth in spite of its not-so-glamourous way of managing customer satisfaction?

2. How does Amway carry out its market survey and competitive intelligence and simultaneously meet its CSR obligations?

SECTION II
CASE STUDIES IN FINANCE MANAGEMENT

Financial Accounting, Direct/Indirect Taxation, Banking, and Insurance

10

Wrong Signals for Investment Climate

A Case Study on Retrospective Taxation (Vodafone)

Learning Objectives

At times in emerging economies like India, the planners seem to be a bit confused between encouraging foreign direct investments as support to economic growth through business expansion and modernization and simultaneously ensuring that the government exchequer gets its dues as taxes from such investments and their continued global business practices of monetizing part of their investments in equity by share transfers.

While attracting foreign direct investments, the benefits and returns on such investments have to be at par or even better than other countries' similar opportunities for investments, but many foreign investors are not clear about the taxation rules of the incumbent country. And it is also seen the inviting country suddenly seem to have woken up to financial transactions of such foreign investors are able to escape provisions of current taxation rules and feel the sudden necessity to introduce retrospective taxation acts/rules to cover such transactions and claim payments as tax arrears from investors for such transactions. The case in question is one of such incidences wherein Vodafone group, a global telecom company getting into a situation wherein it has to pay as arrears of tax for its international revenue transactions for which as per Vodafone, they are not liable to pay.

There are a few more companies facing such situations (CAIRNS) who have sought relief through International Courts.

For the students and practitioners of direct and indirect taxation, this case study offers some insight for clarity.

Indian Business Case Studies. Srilatha Palekar, Arun Pardhi and Sunanda Jindal, Oxford University Press. © ASM Group of Institutes, Pune, India 2022. DOI: 10.1093/oso/9780192869449.003.0010

Synopsis

Vodafone Group Plc is a British multinational telecommunications company headquartered in London and with its registered office in Newbury,
Berkshire. It is the world's second-largest mobile telecommunications
company measured by both subscribers and 2013 revenues (in each
case behind China Mobile), and had 434 million subscribers as of 31
March 2014.

Vodafone owns and operates networks in 21 countries and has partner
networks in over 40 additional countries. Its Vodafone Global Enterprise
division provides telecommunications and IT services to corporate clients in over 65 countries.

Vodafone has a primary listing on the London Stock Exchange and is
a constituent of the FTSE 100 Index. It had a market capitalization of approximately £89.1 billion as of 6 July 2012, the third largest of any company listed on the London Stock Exchange. It has a secondary listing on
NASDAQ.

Vodafone Essar Limited, formerly known as Hutchison Essar, is a telecom service provider in India that covers 23 telecom circles in India and
is based in Mumbai.

Vodafone holds a 67 per cent stake in Vodafone Essar Limited and
Essar holds the rest 33 per cent stake.

On 11 February 2007, Vodafone agreed to acquire the controlling interest of 67 per cent held by Li Ka Shing Holdings in Hutch-Essar for
US$11.1 billion. The company was valued at US$18.8 billion. The transaction closed on 8 May 2007. Despite the official name being Vodafone
Essar, its products are simply branded 'Vodafone'. It offers both prepaid
and postpaid GSM cellular phone coverage throughout India.

The Case Details

Vodafone Group has entered into arrangements with network operators
in countries where the Group does not hold an equity stake. Under the
terms of these partner market agreements, Vodafone and its partner operators co-operate in the marketing of global products and services with
varying levels of brand association. This strategy enables Vodafone to

implement services in new territories and to create additional value to their partners' customers and to Vodafone's travelling customers without the need for equity investment in these countries.

Our diverse array of holdings ranges from some of the world's biggest port operators and retailers, to property development and infrastructure, to innovative and advanced telecommunications and data services.

Hutchison Whampoa

Hutchison Whampoa Ltd. (HWL) reported turnover of approximately HKD413 billion (US$53 billion) for the year ended 31 December 2013. Some of our achievements include being the world's leading port investor, developer, and operator, the world's leading health and beauty retailer, and a pioneer of leading-edge mobile multimedia telecommunications.

With roots in Hong Kong in the 1800s, HWL's operations now span the globe. The multicultural mix of our executives and staff reflects the diversity and reach of our operations.

Essar

This is a multinational corporation with an annual turnover of US$39 billion and investments in steel, energy, information, and services. It employs more than 73,000 in about 25 countries.

Essar began as a construction company in 1969 and has diversified into manufacturing, services, and retail over the years since then. Over the last decade, it has grown through strategic global acquisitions and partnerships, capturing new markets and discovering new raw material sources.

Today, Essar continues to expand its global footprint, focusing on markets in Asia, Africa, Europe, the Americas, and Australia. Essar invests significantly in the latest technology to drive forward and backward integration in its businesses, and on leveraging synergies between these businesses. It also focuses on in-house research and innovation to be a low-cost manufacturer with high-quality products and innovative customer offerings.

Essar Global Fund (EGFL) is a diversified global investment fund with a diversified portfolio of investments across the sectors of energy, metals and mining, infrastructure, and services. The combined assets of Essar Power and Essar Oil constitute Essar Energy.

Hutchison Max Telecom Ltd. (HMTL)

This is a joint venture between Hutchison Whampoa and the Max Group, was established on 21 February 1992. The license to operate in Mumbai (then Bombay) circle was awarded to Hutchison Max by the Department of Telecommunications (DoT) in November 1994. The cellular service branded 'Max Touch' was launched the same year. Switching and other related equipment were provided by Ericsson and the network was designed, engineered, and set up by Motorola. Hutchison Max entered into the Delhi telecom circle in December 1999, the Kolkata circle in July 2000, and the Gujarat circle in September 2000. Licenses for these circles had initially been awarded by the DoT in 1994, 1997, and 1995, respectively. Between 1992 and 2006, Hutchison acquired interests in all 23 mobile telecom circles of India.

The Judicial Nature of the Case

The case concerns a tax dispute between the Vodafone group and the Indian income tax (IT) authorities over the acquisition by Vodafone International Holdings BV (VIH) (part of the Vodafone group and a company resident for tax purposes in the Netherlands) of the entire share capital of CGP Investments (Holdings) Ltd. (a company incorporated in Hong Kong but resident for tax purposes in the Cayman Islands) on 11 February 2007 for about $11 billion (Rs 55,000 crores) from Hutchison Telecommunications International Ltd (HTIL). CGP, through various intermediate companies/contractual arrangements, controlled 67% of Hutchison Essar Limited (HEL), an Indian company.

The acquisition resulted in Vodafone acquiring control over Hutch-Essar, a joint venture between the Hutchison group and the Essar group, which had obtained telecom licenses to provide cellular telephony in different circles in India in November 1994. Because the sale was supposed to have been made overseas, no taxes were paid in India.

The IT authorities in India contended that the primary aim of this transaction was to acquire 67 per cent controlling interest in Hutchison Essar Limited, a company resident in India. They therefore sought to tax capital gains under Section 9(1)(i) of the Indian Income Tax Act 1961 (2) arising from the sale of the share capital of CGP on the basis that CGP, while not a tax resident in India, holds the underlying Indian asset.

According to the tax authorities, the profit made by Hutchison Hong Kong, while it sold its shares of Hutch-Essar to Vodafone, was generated in India. Therefore, Vodafone, the buyer of the shares, had an obligation to withhold and pay the tax in India, before making the payment to Hutchison. The tax demand was US$2.5 billion. Vodafone contested, stating that neither Vodafone nor Hutch was liable to pay the tax as both the companies were located outside India and the deal happened outside India.

Vodafone filed a writ petition in the Bombay High Court challenging the jurisdiction of the tax authorities. In September 2008, the Bombay High Court held that the transaction was one of transfer of capital assets situated in India, and accordingly, the Indian IT authorities had jurisdiction over the matter. It concluded that it would be simplistic to assume that the entire transaction between HTIL and VIH was fulfilled merely upon the transfer of a single share of CGP in the Cayman Islands.

The two-judge bench noted that 'The commercial and business understanding between the parties postulated that what was being transferred from HTIL to VIH BV was the controlling interest in HEL.... HEL was at all times intended to be the target company and a transfer of the controlling interest in HEL was the purpose which was achieved by the transaction' (BS News Paper).

The Supreme Court Verdict

The case went up to the Supreme Court and, based on two keys but independent arguments, the highest court concluded that there was no merit in the High Court's verdict. The first line of reasoning was that the transaction between Vodafone and Hutch was a share transfer (sale) rather than a transfer of capital assets and that the ownership of the capital assets remained vested in the Indian company.

The judgement took recourse to the legal distinction between a company and its shareholders and thus, the judgement does not make a distinction between shareholding that constituted a controlling interest and that which was a pure financial investment. Consequently, it becomes completely immaterial in this specific case that the share(s) actually transferred were not of the company located in India but of offshore companies that ultimately controlled the shares that constituted the controlling interest in the Indian company.

Even if the shares were of a company located in India, in the court's view, it would not have constituted a transfer of capital assets. Once it is accepted that the shareholders of a company have a legal identity distinct from the company, no matter what the proportion of shares they hold, it follows that the two companies would have distinct identities even if one held a controlling share in the other.

The Supreme Court judgement makes it a point to emphasize that even a subsidiary has an identity that is distinct from its parent holding company.

The second interesting aspect of the Supreme Court judgement is that it argues for a 'look at' test in which tax authorities consider the entire Hutchison structure as it existed, 'holistically', at its face value, and not adopt a 'dissecting approach'. In other words, authorities should not ask whether the transaction is a tax avoidance method but apply the 'look at' test to ascertain its legal nature.

The Supreme Court was not in favour of the High Court's 'look through' test because, it claimed, this was inconsistent with the need for certainty and consistency of tax policies that are crucial for taxpayers' confidence (especially foreign investors). The judgement argues that such a going behind the 'corporate veil' or looking through would be legitimate only in cases where it can be established that there is a deliberate intention of evading taxes. In the Supreme Court's view, no such inference can be made in this case if the steps that led to the creation of the complex holding structure of Vodafone and the eventual Vodafone-Hutch transaction were seen in the proper context.

According to the court, the structuring of the transfer of control from Hutch to Vodafone was not done with the specific intention of avoiding taxes. Hence the corporate veil need not be pierced and the fact that there was a transfer of control from Hutch to Vodafone must be ignored. And thus, the tax authorities should concern themselves only with the corporate structure of a merger deal, and not of what assets are changing hands. The court also felt as Vodafone has been doing business in India for a long-time intention of avoiding capital gains tax is not visible.

The Underlying Issues Involved

Why 'look at' and not 'look through'?

The first interesting issue that arises is why authorities should (a) look at (b)and not look through the transactions, especially if what is being examined are complex transactions of mammoth corporations like Vodafone? After all, even simple cases of wrongdoing may not be caught out without looking at the substance of the act beyond the mere form of what is being claimed by the parties.

The Cayman Islands are a small area and it is famous for notorious activities and a safe area for pirates and deserters in yesteryears. Transactions in these areas should normally be viewed with suspicion that has not been taken into consideration in the case.

Amendment Which Created the Issue

Key Budget Provisions Affecting Mergers and Acquisition and Corporate Restructuring

The Finance Bill, 2012 ('Bill' or 'Budget') is out and has attracted a lot of attention, especially to the enforcement provisions and the retrospective amendments. An attempt has been made in this note to identify, compile, and comment on provisions that are likely to have an effect on mergers and acquisitions and corporate restructuring exercises post-enactment of this Bill.

1. A retrospective change taxing the indirect transfer of shares of an Indian Company. Clause 47 (iv)

Section 9 of the IT provides cases of income, which are deemed to accrue or arise in India. This is a legal fiction created to tax income, which may or may not arise in India and would not have been taxable but for the deeming provision created by this section. Sub-section (1) (i) provides a set of circumstances in which income accruing or arising, directly or indirectly, is taxable in India.

One of the limbs of clause (i) is income accruing or arising directly or indirectly through the transfer of a capital asset situated in India. The legislative intent of this clause through this budgetary amendment is to widen the application as it covers incomes, which are accruing or arising directly or indirectly out of the assets/investments in India to the person resident outside India. The section codifies the source rule of taxation wherein the state, where the actual economic nexus of income is situated, has a right to tax the income irrespective of the place of residence of the entity deriving the income.

Where corporate structure is created to route funds, the actual gain or income arises only in consequence of the investment made in the activity to which such gains are attributable and not the mode through which such gains are realized. Thus, the source country has taxation right on the gains derived from offshore transactions where the value is attributable to the underlying assets.

Current Position

Vodafone Group has already begun an international arbitration against the Indian government in the more than Rs 20,000 crores tax case. The Indian government has appointed former Chief Justice of India R.C. Lahoti as arbitrator in the tax dispute.

The arbitration stems from a tax dispute over Vodafone's acquisition of Hutchison Whampoa's Indian assets in 2007. The government has maintained that the transaction is taxable because it involves Indian assets. Vodafone says Indian tax laws don't apply as the transaction occurred between two overseas companies.

In 2012, the Supreme Court ruled that Vodafone was not liable to pay taxes on its acquisition. Later that year, the government changed rules to enable it to tax deals that had already been concluded.

The government's initial tax demand of Rs 7,990 crores in 2007 has now risen to nearly Rs 20,000 crores because of interests and penalties.

Uncertainties over tax policy in India have unsettled investors, and tax claims on foreign companies have been a major concern. IBM Corp, Royal Dutch Shell Plc, and Nokia are among foreign firms contesting local tax claims.

In the context of the above and present need for improving investors climate in the country, can the government do away with certain laws or has Vodafone taken the matter too far is a question that comes to the mind of a common citizen. So the following questions can help to clear the air in this regard.

Case Questions

1. How is the case of taxation of the accrued interest on two foreign organizations completing an acquisition deal of their assets in a third country looked into by International Courts?

2. Why is Vodafone not exiting from the Indian market in spite of huge alleged tax liability? Do they feel that they have a weaker case? Why did they offer to make an out-of-court settlement of the claimed tax dues from IT?

3. What is likely to be a global investments impact for fresh FII or FDI in India in view of the above case? What are the likely consequences if the case is settled either way? What according to you would be a win–win resolution for both the parties involved?

11

Managing Investments through PE Funds

A Case Study in Financial Risk Management

Learning Objectives

There is a rat race happening between PE investors to catch on to equally fast pace of various start-ups and ventures in the service sector, attracting small but several investments opportunities with highly lucrative returns on valuations.

Many promoters are also jumping in the que to make fast bucks by investing in their own business and turning out to be partners in VE funds and enjoying a double whammy both as promoters as also Investors.

However, the real heat is felt by the employees and other vendors as major stakeholders whose careers and employment uncertainties are pushing them to kick up frequent job switches or labour unrests landing up in courtroom battles.

This has also led to serious conflicts between PE fund Investors and the promoters getting stuck in deals resulting in disastrous losses and un-ending IR issues turning violent at times.

This case study picks up a few such PE investors and promoters' perils as also including corrupt practices by passing regulatory norms laid out on capital taxes and other compliance requirements and resulting in chaos and disbelief.

Indian Business Case Studies. Srilatha Palekar, Arun Pardhi and Sunanda Jindal, Oxford University Press. © ASM Group of Institutes, Pune, India 2022. DOI: 10.1093/oso/9780192869449.003.0011

Synopsis

While India appears to be one of the very attractive opportunities for PE investors, both domestic and international economic opportunities, the ground realities belie such understandings in view of major squabbles between the promoters and PE investors. This leads to the feeling of financial risks for the PE investors who hesitate for such investments.

Case Details

Three senior executives walk into a restaurant. They run this restaurant as a joint venture and they are here to meet some disgruntled employees. The employees refuse to meet them separately and demand a collective meeting on the kitchen floor. The executives agree.

In a few minutes, the conversation turns into a heated argument. The lights on the kitchen floor go out, and the assembled employees jump on the executives and start thrashing them. After a few minutes, the executives manage to flee, through the customer area and to their car parked outside. The angry employees give chase, land some more blows on the three executives and their car.

It looks like a scene from a Bollywood film. It's a first information report (FIR) filed by one of those executives—Puneet Varma, assistant vice-president (operations) of Sagar Ratna Restaurants Private Limited, which runs one of India's largest South-Indian food chains. The incident happened at Ashok Hotel, a five-minute walk from the residence of the prime minister of India, alleges the FIR.

The three executives were appointed by India Equity Partners (IEP), the private equity (PE) firm that acquired 75% of Sagar Ratna Restaurants for Rs 180 crores from original promoter Jayaram Banan in 2011. Those were better times in this promoter–PE relationship.

Today, IEP sees Banan, who remains a significant minority stakeholder, as a troublemaker, violating a non-compete agreement and working from the inside to harm the business. 'Banan instigated some of his people to beat up our management', alleges an IEP spokesperson.

And Banan sees IEP as an inept manager of the business he built. Denying all charges, he says: 'They (IEP) have destroyed the company.

I will file cases against them at the appropriate time'. That refrain of a broken relationship between PE and promoters—is showing up in uncomfortable doses in India Inc and is finding expression in multiple ways.

PE firm Bain Capital and garment company Lilliput Kidswear have ended up in court. Lilliput wanted to stop Bain from selling its stake. Bain alleged Lilliput was fudging its accounts and sending threatening text messages to its representatives, which promoter Narula denied. They are supposed to feed off each other, with promoters bringing in business acumen and PE supplying capital and advice.

But increasingly, in India, in the backdrop of a tough operating environment and a limping regulatory framework, PE firms are feeding on each other. The charges are many such as accounting fraud, diversion of funds, contract violation, etc.

The IEP-Banan dispute, for example, centres around the contours of competition. At the time of sale, the agreement was that Banan would not start another restaurant business for seven years. However, IEP claims Banan is behind a competing South-Indian food chain, Shree Rathnam, which has 26 outlets across India. 'He has set up a competing chain with his nephew, who worked in the business for 20 years and resigned a few weeks after we took over', the IEP spokesperson says. 'He is completely behind it. Every supplier we have come across has told us that Banan is behind that business'. Counters Banan: 'I have no connection with Shree Rathnam at all'.

When it comes to promoter–PE conflicts, India is not an outlier. Where India is different is the nature of these conflicts and how they tend to play out. The conflicts are, increasingly, becoming more acrimonious, even farcical, less professional, and more personal. They are shining an ugly light on promoter quality and business practices, which were never of the highest order in India, and the unfavourable regulations. 'Promoters have used regulatory hurdles against PE investors', says Sanjeev Krishan, executive director of audit and consulting firm Price Waterhouse Coopers. 'This is one reason why the number of active PE funds has come down in India'.

The genesis of this friction goes back, ironically, to a good time— between 2005 and 2008. 'Many of the current disputes relate to investments made in the pre-financial meltdown of 2008, when liquidity was aplenty and PE investors were like a person with a hammer looking for a nail', says Shriram Subramanian, founder and MD, InGovern Research Services, a proxy advisory firm. 'They went around making investments without much credence to valuations and/or promoter quality. They also turned a blind eye to many questionable business practices of their investee firms'.

Due diligence was a 'tick in the box item' during those three years (2005–08), says Krishan of PwC. 'It was an auction like process with over-exuberance'. A proper due diligence takes at least four to eight weeks, depending on the size of the company, and costs anywhere between Rs 15 lakhs and Rs 30 lakhs, according to Jamil Khatri, global head of accounting advisory services for KPMG. During those days, he adds, audit firms were forced to complete the process in half the time.

Khatri, who has examined the books of some companies that received PE investments, says due diligence should focus on three aspects: aggressive accounting practices where revenues were proactively accounted for and expenses were not shown, related-party transactions, and quality of audit. Besides going over a company's accounts with a forensic comb, this entails running a background check on promoters and their dealings with other stakeholders, ascertaining the genuineness of vendors and customers, and looking critically at disputes.

A consultant with a multinational accounting firm who has done due diligence for PE firms highlights one of the ways in which promoters add gloss. 'Promoters have access to cash through their family circles', he says, not wanting to be named. 'They route this cash via fictitious companies to show as genuine payments for sales done. The cash comes into the company, but it is just to boost sales and profitability, and paint a rosy picture'.

When asked what due diligence IEP did before investing in Sagar Ratna, its spokesperson says: 'The due diligence has been pretty thorough, but obviously not thorough enough... The top firms do not use anyone but the Big Four (accounting firms). The issue is: if a promoter is determined to do a Satyam Computer style gamble on you, what are you going to do?' In recent conflicts, 'promoters have come out poorly', adds the consultant quoted above. 'Controls are just not there. Few people control the entire operations and they resist change'.

Rituraj Sinha bristles when such observations are made in a sweeping way. 'All promoters cannot be tarred with the same brush', says Sinha, group chief operating officer, Security and Intelligence Services (India). 'PE funds are in the business of investing and identifying well-run businesses from the bad ones. Therefore, the onus is on them'.

This April, SIS raised Rs 500 crores from PE firm CX Partners, and in the process, gave its previous risk-capital backer, global hedge fund DE Shaw, a seven-fold return on its Rs 20 crores investment made in 2008. But exits for PE funds—who, typically, invest with a four- to seven-year period have been few and far between since 2008, when economies and markets collapsed. According to Vikram Gupta, founder and managing partner of Ivy Cap Ventures Advisors, a PE fund, says there were only 450 exits between 2009 and 2012.

It remains to be seen how the RBI views allowing options. In the past, the RBI has raised reservations against buyback clauses—a standard clause in most shareholder agreements in investments in real estate companies. Its argument is that a buyback makes it a quasi-debt investment, not equity, and that foreign borrowings are banned in real estate.

Alok Mittal, managing partner of Canaan India, a venture capital firm, says such clauses (guaranteeing return through promoter or company buyback) have not been substantially implemented, and PE funds would stay longer if they see a company performing well. Raja Lahiri, partner with Grant Thornton, says the clauses are getting re-negotiated or sometimes extended, and private equity are looking at secondary deals to exit.

Another irritant cited by PE is the delay in resolving conflicts through the Indian legal system. 'It takes an inordinate amount of time for the courts to do anything', says the IEP spokesperson. 'If you are going to get anything after eight or 10 years of ongoing litigation, you may as well not bother with having any enforceability'. Adds Mukherjee. 'The game now is to get interim relief. People know it will take time to get the final order. So, parties are protecting their rights by securing interim relief'.

According to the IEP spokesperson, India has regulations, but they don't get enforced because of corruption. IEP says it is not yet exploring selling off Sagar Ratna, former promoter Banan has offered to buy it at a 25% markdown to the sale price—but its hands are full managing the business, and negotiating the contractual and legal disputes related to its two-year-old investment.

Case Questions

1. On one hand, Indian government wants to promote private investment funds to invest in business, whereas the PE funds find it difficult to operate through such investments due basically to inadequate legal protection to their investments resulting in frequent bickering and legal complications. How according to you such issues be resolved?

2. Are Indian promoters playing fair in their commitments to the PE partners or are they always in a way suspicious of PE investors' intentions of fair financial objectives of the investments? Who is to blame for the rut that gets created in the majority of such instances?

12

Jet Airways from 'Rise' to Steep 'Fall'

Learning Objectives

To critically analyse the success factors of Jet Airways and the reasons for its fall. To provide a base for understanding the impact of socio-cultural, political impact on the working of a business. To understand the practical difficulties of airline companies in India. This case can be used for postgraduate and undergraduate management students to analyse the various financial, management and entrepreneurial reasons for the fall of Jet Airways in India in spite of Indian aviation being one of the most promising markets for the airline Industry.

Synopsis

Jet Airways, a brainchild of visionary and excellent entrepreneur Naresh Goyal, incorporated in 1992, started taxi operations in 1993, began full operations by 1995 and got permission to fly international flights by aviation ministry to London in 2004. Naresh Goyal had vast experience in the field of aviation before entering the market. He availed the opportunity floored by the Government of India by liberalizing the Indian market and started Jet Airways and took various decisions at the correct point of time, which helped Jet Airways to lead the aviation market of India from 1997 to 2009. It was the leading airline of India, providing excellent services to its customers and making a strong, loyal customer base. It had a trained pilot and crew members to suit the needs of the concepts of the airline.

Introduction of low-cost airline in the Indian airline industry, rising fuel prices and mechanism to handle its impact, understanding the norm

Indian Business Case Studies. Srilatha Palekar, Arun Pardhi and Sunanda Jindal, Oxford University Press. © ASM Group of Institutes, Pune, India 2022. DOI: 10.1093/oso/9780192869449.003.0012

of market and hesitation and inability to break the image of the airline as Luxury service provider made Jet Airways suffer and finally grounding its flights. The negligence of banks and regulators and their approach in the future towards debt-ridden companies would decide the future of Jet Airways.

Indian Airline industry had witnessed different phases, from premium class service for rich and prestigious people to services for middle-income groups resulting in enhancing a huge customer base. This case analyses the journey of Jet Airways from a vision to the leader and its fall. This case tries to analyse the various milestone steps taken in the way of a successful journey and the hasty decisions and wrong intentions which lead to the fall of such a successful and glorious Indian aircraft.

Airline companies in India have been working since post-independence. The first airline service started between Naini and Allahabad to carry mails during Kumbh Mela. Slowly it took place as a luxury mode of transportation among higher-income groups. After independence, some private airlines were merged and national carrier 'Indian Airlines' was made under the public sector. Airlines were far from the reach of common middle-class people of India. The aviation sector had seen different phases in India after liberalization in 1991, and its demand had been increasing at a faster pace, many domestic and international players got attracted towards entering the airline market, more and more customers are attracted towards airline services. This case talks about Jet Airways, a leading airline company in India for many decades, from inception till its end. Jet Airways is the brainchild of visionary entrepreneur Naresh Goyal, who started his venture in 1992, firstly as taxi operations in 1993, by 1995 Jet Airways began its full services in the airline industry of India. They got permission to fly internationally by aviation ministry to London in 2004. It gave premium class services to the fliers and was a premium brand of Indian private airline services. The growth of the economy and income in the hands of the middle-income group gave a boost to the airline industry of India. The middle class and lower middle class of India are switching towards airlines in order to save time; the growing income in the hands of this sector of the population had given a boom to the business of the airline industry.

The case describes the crisis of Jet Airways and its history with the current situation of Indian airlines industry and looks forward to answering questions on whether the problems in Airline industries should be re-solved by putting forth some resolution plans to the government should opt for regulatory actions.

Case Details

Indian Aviation markets contributed around $72 billion by 2018–2019 to GDP. India has 464 airports and airstrips, among which Airport Authority of India owns 125 airports. Passenger demand (RPK) had been Rs. 80966 m in 2015–2016, Rs. 98641m in 2016–2017 and 117042 in 2017–2018 with a passenger load increasing from 82.8% to 84.3% to 87% as per the data of DGCA, the regulator of the aviation sector. India had 594 scheduled and 214 non-scheduled flights in 2017–2018. Various new initiatives like low-cost carrier, FDI, Modern airport of Delhi, Mumbai, Hyderabad, advance IT interventions, new locations, better technology in aircraft, and air control is approaching the Indian market. The aviation industry consists of manufacturing and operations of all types of aircraft.

Jet Airways is the brainchild of an excellent visionary and entrepreneur Naresh Goyal, who had worked on almost every segment of the aviation industry, from being a cashier to travel agency, to handling PR of an inter-national airline, to negotiating for the purchase of aircraft before entering into his own venture. Starting with his journey, Naresh Goyal belonged to a lower-middle-class family of Patiala, owning jewellery businesses that were under a lot of debt after his father's death. He completed his B.Com in 1966 and started working as a cashier in his relative's travel agency in Connaught Place, Delhi. His exposure to the airline industry started from here.

He worked under his uncle in a travel agency and gained knowledge, expertise, and connections with national and internationally important people of this segment. He also worked for Iraq Airlines as PR Manager and for Middle Eastern Airlines for ticketing, reservations, etc. Jordan Airlines hired him to open an office in Delhi and his work gave him an opportunity to negotiate for buying aircraft in Malaysia for extension of Jordan Airways business. This is when he met the MD of Jordan Airline, Mr. Ali Gantur, who trusted him and helped him to make connections in the Indian and international aviation industry.

By 1974, he had made good connections and an experience of working in almost every grass root to the upper level of the aviation industry; this helped him to enter the airline business with maximum preparations.

In 1974, he launched a travel agency, Jet Air and in the year 1991 with the liberalization of the market he planned to avail the opportunities and Jet Airways was founded by Naresh Goyal as a limited liability company on 27 April 1992 where Tail Winds had capital investment, which was a company registered in Isle of Man. Jet Airways initially started with air taxi as the government did not allow private scheduled carriers; Air India was holding the market by this time.

In 1993, with some relaxations in government policies in the aviation sector, Jet Airways started its services with 2 Boeing 737-300 planes. By the year 2002, Jet Airways was capable of crossing Indian airlines' market share.

In December 2004, Jet Airways went public and its first IPO came in February 2005, offering 20% of the airline's stock, which was highly welcomed by investors and raised 18.9 billion for Jet Airways. In the year 2005, Jet got permission for international flight to Hitherto, London. Jet airways ruled the market with its premium quality services, loyal customer, customer-centric approach; it was a market leader between 2006 and 2009.

2005 was the year when low-cost carriers entered the Indian Aviation sector and became popular as per the rising growth of middle-income group, under certain conditions, Jet Airways decided to enter low-cost sector by acquiring Air Sahara in 2005 for Rs. 1,450 corers, which was not performing well, Jet launched Jet Lite by merging Air Sahara.

This initially looked as a wise decision but gradually, it came out to be a big mistake of Naresh Goyal, when Jet Airways was already fighting with a tough time, it acquired another burden in the form of Air Sahara, which actually increased the burden the relieving. Air Sahara brought many legal, financial, and HR issues with it which impacted Jet Airways in the long run.

In the year 2008, Jet Airways made an alliance with competitor Kingfisher for code sharing to perform in frequent flyer programme. The entry of low-cost airlines like Indigo, SpiceJet, GoAir compelled the giants like Kingfisher and Jet Airways to think of reducing the cost as their passenger market share was slowly drifting. In 2009, Jet Airways launched Jet Connect for small routes.

Later, Jet Lite and Jet Connect were merged. Some strong decisions were taken by the airline to fight back as to reduce the prices of tickets without reducing the expensive and extensive service provided by them. By 2010, Jet Airways was holding 22.6% of the passenger market share.

Jet Airways captured the market from 2010 as the largest carrier by passenger market share till 2012. In 2011, the airline banned meat products and liquids in its aircraft. The year 2012 came as hope to giant airlines struggling with stiff completion given by low-cost airlines, when government announced that foreign airlines could take up to 49% stake in Indian carriers.

Availing the opportunity, Jet announced the selling of 24% of its shares to Etihad Airlines and retaining 51% with Naresh Goyal. In November 2013, Jet airline sold its 24% stake in US$379 million to Etihad. This deal created a problem between Star Alliance and Jet Airways, Star Alliance cancelled its deal with Jet Airways and opened the path for Air India.

The market was throwing new challenges for leaders like low-cost airlines, international players, government regulations, FDI, etc. to cope with. By this time, Jet was looking forward to expanding in the international market. Roaring fuel prices were a big problem for the Indian airline industry; it was calling for a hedging policy that was not taken care of by Jet Airways. The airline industry was yet thought to be a luxury sector that needed to be taken care of by the government by this time, high airport charges, landing and take-off charges, allotment of prime time, and schedule of flying had been very ambiguous, with many players in the market it was tuff to compete by now.

By October 2017, it was the second-largest airline in India after Indigo, with 17.8% passenger market share, which fell to 15.5% by 2018 in comparison to 22.5% in 2015. February 2019 jet announced to withdraw services from 9 Indian and Gulf airports to concentrate on its hubs.

Jet Airways was India's leading airline, which was one of the finest service providers with great customer loyalty and had overcome many hurdles on its journey towards success had suddenly stopped due to several reasons. Naresh Goyal wrote to the Travel Agents Association of India, stating they are cutting down on uneconomical routes and shifting towards more profitable routes.

By the end of 2017–2018, Indigo became the leader in terms of domestic demand market share in terms of RPK and passenger carrier with

40.9% and Jet Airlines had 14.6% market share, followed by SpiceJet and Air India. Whereas in International scheduled carriers, Jet was holding a 13.8% market share as a leader.

Jet Airways (India) Ltd Share Holding as on 31 March 2019

Category	No. of Shares	Percentage
Promoters	1,000	0.00
No. of shares	113,597,383	100.00
Foreign promoter	57,933,665	51.00
Others	33,485,226	29.48
General public	13,820,994	12.17
NBFC and mutual funds	4,068,463	3.58
Financial institutions	2,617,519	2.30
Foreign institutions	1,670,516	1.47

Source: *Economic Times*.

Please refer Annexure for P&L statement.

The financial records of Jet Airways were alarming in the last five years about its health. The company had a debt of Rs. 8,000 crores. The records were reflecting capital of around 14,000 crores, the liability of 20,000 crores, and assets worth 12,000 crores. Planes were grounded for non-payment of lease, fuel delivery stopped, flights cancelled, and salary of staff was not given.

Jet Airways requested interim funding to SBI lead consortium of banks, which banks denied, and no other lender was ready for emergency funding; due to this, Jet Airways was unable to pay fuel and critical services to keep operations running and had to shut down all its domestic and international flights.

The consortium of banks led by SBI came into the picture. They asked in March 2019 Naresh Goyal and his family to step down as chairman and board of directors to revive the conditions of Jet Airways expecting. The banks having a bad experience with Kingfisher were not ready to infuse more funds.

Finally, on 18 April 2019, all flights were cancelled by Jet Airways. It was announced through a notice to BSE that the consortium of banks is not ready to infuse more funds in Jet.

The employees of Jet Airways are coming forward and asking government to infuse funds for this debt-ridden company and save the jobs of 20,000 employees.

Gaining an edge

Airlines' yields are likely to jump in Q4 FY19 because of the disruption in Jet Airways' operations.

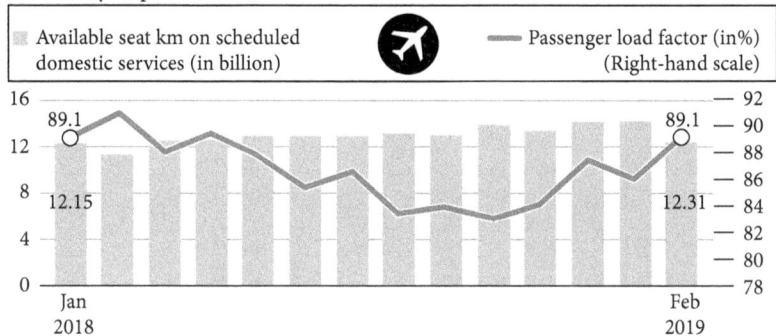

Banks were looking forward to investors for the sale of Jet, but the question arises what they have as assets; most of their planes were acquired by leasing, which is voided because of non-payment.

The only thing left as asset is their landing and take-off time slot at Mumbai and Delhi airports which was allotted to some airlines to fill the gaps by the government. The sale in process on 10 May 2019 had only one investor for the beleaguered airline, Etihad who already had a 24% stake in Jet and wanted limited liability restricted to its share and other conditions too, as Etihad had burnt its hand with the bankruptcy of Air Berlin and Alitalia in 2017 had not shown much interest.

Case Questions

1. What went wrong with Jet Airways?

2. Should banks or government infuse money in Jet Airways or take it to bankruptcy?

3. What would be the major challenges faced by investors willing to invest in Jet Airways?

Annexure

Profit and Loss—Jet Airways (India) Ltd. Rs (in Crores)

	Mar'18	Mar'17	Mar'16	Mar'15	Mar'14
	12 months	12 months	12 months	12 months	12 months
INCOME:					
Sales turnover	23,286.53	21,552.35	21,167.33	19,573.43	17,301.89
Excise duty	.00	.00	.00	.00	.00
NET SALES	23,286.53	21,552.35	21,167.33	19,573.43	17,301.89
Other income	0	0	0	0	0
TOTAL INCOME	23,958.37	23,040.87	21,910.96	20,280.73	17,713.47
EXPENDITURE:					
Manufacturing expenses	6,953.25	5,473.78	5,015.73	6,686.26	7,175.42
Material consumed	.00	.00	188.58	139.90	121.57
Personal expenses	2,995.35	2,890.01	2,388.13	2,243.00	1,899.59
Selling expenses	.00	.00	.00	.00	.00
Administrative expenses	13,313.96	11,672.77	11,360.60	10,620.22	9,589.96
Expenses capitalized	.00	.00	.00	.00	.00
Provisions made	.00	.00	.00	.00	.00
TOTAL EXPENDITURE	23,262.56	20,036.56	18,953.04	19,689.38	18,786.54
Operating profit	23.97	1,515.79	2,214.29	-115.95	-1,484.65

EBITDA	695.81	3,004.31	2,957.92	591.35	-1073.07
Depreciation	620.57	670.90	995.09	762.50	875.75
Other write-offs	.00	.00	.00	.00	.00
EBIT	75.24	2,333.41	1,962.83	-171.15	-1,948.82
Interest	842.86	851.09	868.11	884.06	997.16
EBT	-767.62	1,482.32	1,094.72	-1,055.21	-2,945.98
Taxes	.00	-.20	.00	.00	-.12
Profit and loss for the year	-767.62	1,482.52	1,094.72	-1,055.21	-2,945.86
Non-recurring items	.00	.00	78.84	-758.50	-721.99
Other non-cash adjustments	.00	.00	.00	.00	.00
Other adjustments	.00	.00	.00	.00	.00
REPORTED PAT	-767.62	1,482.52	1,173.56	-1,813.71	-3,667.85
KEY ITEMS					
Preference dividend	.00	.00	.00	.00	.00
Equity dividend	.00	.00	.00	.00	.00
Equity dividend (%)	.00	.00	.00	.00	.00
Shares in issue (lakhs)	1,135.97	1,135.97	1,135.97	1,135.97	1,135.97
EPS—Annualized (Rs)	-67.57	130.51	103.31	-159.66	-322.88

Source: https://economictimes.indiatimes.com/jet-airways-(india)-ltd/profitandlose/companyid-4374.cms

SECTION III

MULTIDISCIPLINARY CASE STUDIES

Marketing, Strategy, Operations

13

Tug of War Between Online and Offline in Retail

A Case Study on Big Bazaar and Flipkart

Learning Objectives

The line 'Everything is fair in love and war' is very suitable for the tug of war between on and offline in the retail sector as both players of on and off are adopting various marketing strategies to attract and retain the customers and there are clashes of marketing offerings which is making the king of the market-customer delighted. For sustaining and surviving in this global competitive business world, all are in the hurry to differentiate themselves from others by hook or crook and only that would be the market leader who will be the fittest among all. From 'Big Billion Day Sale' on Flipkart to Big Bazaar's 'Saal ka Sabse Sasta Din', the war is on to acquire more and more customers in a short span of time are the current marketing strategies adopted by companies of marketplaces and market spaces.

The key question from a policy point of view is whether this is a momentary or enduring trend as many popular on and offline companies are on the border of failure as they are making losses while very few are successful.

Students in marketing management will find this case study interesting to see how the online and offline retail networks are strengthening their cobwebs to trap major footfalls and customer groups.

Indian Business Case Studies. Srilatha Palekar, Arun Pardhi and Sunanda Jindal, Oxford University Press. © ASM Group of Institutes, Pune, India 2022. DOI: 10.1093/oso/9780192869449.003.0013

Synopsis

In India, it was Mr Kishore Biyani, the promoter of Future group, in-strumental in introducing the mall culture and the offline retail almost a decade ago. Based on the response the Future group received for its off-line retail business, many other major players like the Shoppers Stop, Flip Kart, Aditya Birla group in readymade garments, the Tatas in Trent, and many in fast food retailers have by now crowded the Indian online and offline retail market including now the giant killer Amazon following the Walmart who entered India almost in the early 2000s.

This case study tries to take a sample cut of the warlike situation of se-vere competition now prevalent in Indian offline and online retail and the street fight between Future group and the FlipKart to snatch away each other's customer base by luring with all types of discounts and sales offers including emptying of the waste boxes of customers.

Case Details

India with the second highly populated country, has the great purchasing power, and identifying these golden opportunities, many e-retailers and retailers entered Indian marketplaces, which have been shifted from the real bazaars to the virtual ones, but little has changed between the 2006 Big Bazaar's 'Sabse Sasta Din' to the 'Big Billion Day Sale' online sale by Flipkart. Since ancient times, Indians have been habitual of purchasing products from haats, weekly bazaars, street hawkers, and kirana stores.

With the change in time, the traders changed the way of selling prod-ucts by adopting retail stores like supermarkets and this made traditional brick-and-mortar retailers bothered about their future and existence. As we know very well that change is the law of nature and nothing is constant and hence the marketplaces are transforming themselves as per the need of the hour.

Big Bazaar

The India's leading supermarket having over 200 stores across India, is the chain of retail stores of the big banner Pantaloon Retail (India) Ltd., headed by Kishore Biyani. The company is doing very well as a traditional brick-and-mortar retailer and touching new milestones every day. Promotional scheme offerings like Sabse Sasta Din, Wednesday Bazaar, 5 Days Maha Bachat, Public Holiday sale, and many more are innovative ways to drag potential traffic of customers in the stores. With the transformation in new technologies, the marketing teleported itself to digital platforms and this gave birth to online retailers like Amazon, Flipkart, Alibaba, Snapdeal, and many more.

Previously there was a tug of war among retailers and kirana stores in which retailers were more successful. Nowadays, online retailers are becoming more aggressive in promotional activities to attract, acquire, and retain customers rather than retailers and hence are generating more businesses.

Flipkart

Flipkart, an e-commerce company, founded in 2007 by Sachin Bansal and Binny Bansal, is very successful in online retailing through various schemes and offers at regular intervals of time. Creating brand visibility and generating revenues through various promotional initiatives such as Big Billion Day Sale, Freedom Sale, Flipkart Fashion Sale, and many more.

There were some identified gaps between both of and online retailers, which led to tug war among them. These are mentioned as below:

1. Online vs. offline—Online has no any geographical limitation while offline has limited geographical boundary.
2. Impersonal vs. personal—Customers are unknown to online and they even don't visit the company while offline; customers are known as many of them are regular visitors and they know about the company.
3. Reverse logistics vs. no return—In online, there was great return of products which is increasing reverse logistics costing while there is no any return in offline and in some cases only replacement within a certain period of time.
4. Limited choices vs. much more choice—Customers have limited choice on online and have much more choice available at offline.

5. Login vs. footfall—Customers are visiting the company websites more but placing less orders out which many orders are cancelled while in footfall, the conversion is more as the customer believes more in reality than virtuality.
6. Quality vs. cost-quality may be good in online retail while the price of product is higher in offline than online.

Big Bazaar visualized the upcoming opportunities of online retailing to make an additional business from online by starting its new venture Big Bazaar Direct to compete with online retailers like Flipkart, Amazon, etc.

The above factors are the major hurdles in the path of offline retailers due to which they are facing tough competition from online retail giants. The business model of online retailers is better than offline retailers.

Nowadays, customers are buying more through online after doing the research before buying. Prices at online are low in comparison to offline. Hence there are increases in the number of online retailers as they don't have to rent stores, no need to pay VAT, no need for storing the stock as they simply deliver goods from the seller to the customer.

Many Offline Retailers Are Closing Their Stores as They Are Not Able to Make Profits

The PwC Global Report (2013–2014) on multichannel retailing points out that the physical store has historically proven to be a 'powerful, long-lived and adaptable institution. While in India, the online retail has become popular only over the past few years, online retail has been a part of the global retail industry for almost a decade now. Despite this, global online retail constitutes only about 8% to 10% of the total retail.

As a country with an emerging online retail category, India has a lot to learn from the global growth route of the e-commerce and e-tailing industry. On being polled regarding reasons why consumers shop in-store, respondents consistently voted for factors that are unique to physical stores, such as the ability to see, touch, and try the merchandise; immediate availability of the product; and being more certain about fit or suitability of the product. These factors also received an increased percentage of the respondents' votes, as compared to last year's data.

When e-commerce sites made shopping for us as easy as a click, we all thought that there is no looking back. Well, not always. The e-commerce giant Amazon ran into trouble with a high-end kitchen knife manufacturer, Wüsthof. It stopped selling through Amazon because it realized that price-cutting at Amazon could give a short-term jump in sales, but in the long term, it may mean erosion of margins and closure of retail shops, which drive the sales process of a new line of products. What this tells us is that things are not just black and white. If we look at the retail sector, both the offline and online spheres are now beginning to intersect. It's no longer a question of online vs. offline; consumers want to be able to shop in-store or online, whenever they want, wherever they are. They want to experience products as well as have the comfort of ordering them sitting at home. It's all about what they want.

Many online start-ups are realizing the benefits of having an offline presence. Both online start-ups and brick-and-mortar stores are looking at ways to give customers a seamless shopping experience. Also, online players are creating offline experience zones where customers can have a look and feel of the product. All of us have seen Urban Ladder and Pepperfry furniture displayed at Indian airports. For a certain type of product category, it makes sense to have a strategy where the customer experiences the product, especially the newly launched sub-product line, at a physical store and then places order by browsing through a digital catalogue in the same store. This presents a scenario where both the customer and the brand experience best of both worlds, online and offline.

Now that online sales are growing at approximately 10 times the rate of brick and mortar, it comes as no surprise when savvy retailers like Macy's start beefing up their e-commerce capabilities. Today's consumers live multi-dimensional, multi-platform lives—and their buying behaviours reflect that same complex dynamic. In many ways, retailers are now racing to catch up. Retail sectors, which have been generating plenty of employment opportunities for the people and revenues to the government, are facing many problems related to marketing. Without overcoming those problems, it is not easy for them to sustain themselves in the market. Hence to sustain in the market, survival is essential and for this change is the need of the hour. The point of purchase is losing its significance in this Omni-channel environment. The focus is on showcasing your product to the customer in the best possible way and selling it at a competitive price.

Whether the sale happens over the counter or through a click will depend on the customer. Indian retail sector is in the phase of transformation from offline to online and this is a good sign for the market as it is beneficial for the customers. The tug of war between the retail industries has created a new history as there is price war and showering of offers in the market and make the customer delighted. Once the retailers understand their customers in a better way, once they know what makes them tick, they will be able to put the right package before them, whether that's online or offline.

Case Questions

1. Whether this is a momentary or enduring trend as many popular online and offline companies are on the border of failure as they are making losses and profits due to their tug of war through market offerings?

2. 'Will this war is good for the market?' Comment on it with your statement. What markets do you see emerging in the sector? How can the marketer know what the customers most want?

3. Is Big Bazaar's decision to enter in online retailing a good one? How is it beneficial in the long run?

4. Can retailers become just as multi-dimensional? Is it possible for them to be all things to all people? Which are the most desirable options for customers?

14

Understanding the Indian Customer

A Case Study on Typical Indian Customer Behaviour

Learning Objectives

Understanding Indian customer behaviour and customer experience have ever been an interesting topic and task for many global business entities who, after having been in India for decades, are not clear of the customer expectations and behaviour so peculiar to the Indian subcontinent, especially with thousands of castes and cultural inhibitions which make it extremely difficult for someone who has been otherwise successful elsewhere finds it difficult to succeed equally in Indian markets. The automobile giants of the world, you may name anyone who has invested in India with high hopes of capturing a major market share, have not been able to exceed 5 per cent of the huge Automobile market in India. The same applies to many more market and industry segments in India.

The case deals with some peculiar aspects related to Indian ethos and customer behaviour for goods and services.

Synopsis

It is said that as one travels east, the rising sun inhibits glare on the eyes and makes people to have smaller eyes as also appear at times indifferent to glamour and shiny objects. But in business parlance, many big businesses from the western world find this curious since they find it difficult to easily access eastern markets in spite of their superior convincing power and claimed technical superiority.

Indian Business Case Studies. Srilatha Palekar, Arun Pardhi and Sunanda Jindal, Oxford University Press. © ASM Group of Institutes, Pune, India 2022. DOI: 10.1093/oso/9780192869449.003.0014

It has been ages that many global auto giants have been trying their best of business acumen to claim major Indian auto market share but many of them, in spite of years of experimentation, have not dented any reasonable presence in Indian markets.

Whether the above could be related to peculiar mindsets and preferences of Indian customer is a debatable issue but the facts confirm that there is something peculiar in the buying behaviour of Indian customers.

Case Details

Customer understanding is a must-have, especially during hard times. Today, the first thing a company that considers itself truly global does is say goodbye to the practice of dumping products and services developed for one market in its next. South Korean automotive manufacturer Hyundai Motor Company (HMC) is a case in point. With an investment in the region of Rs 182 crores, the company opened its R&D centre in India in Hyderabad during the economic slowdown of 2009. The reason: strengthen India's position as an R&D and manufacturing hub.

Says Rakesh Srivastava, senior vice-president (sales and marketing), Hyundai Motor India (HMI), 'When we entered the country the passenger car segment was largely price-driven. This was the time when owning a car was considered a luxury. Today buying a car is about making a statement and when that happens leading companies must bring state-of-the-art technology and design to its customers at the same time globally'. HMI claims that a large chunk of market research work is conducted by its in-house teams. For Hyundai, there was no other alternative really.

'For multinationals, the key to reaching the next level will be learning to do business the Indian way, rather than simply imposing global business models and practices on the local market', write authors Vimal Choudhary, Alok Kshirsagar, and Ananth Narayanan in a McKinsey & Company article (How Multinationals Can Win in India, March 2012) (ET News Paper). 'It's a lesson many companies have already learned in China, which more multinationals are treating as a second home market. In India, this trend has been slower to pick up steam ...' (the article mentions). Yes, they have been slower but it is happening nonetheless.

Coming back to Hyundai, the company has a four-layer market research strategy in place. It all starts with a brand track study which assesses Hyundai's performance vis-à-vis other players on parameters like brand connect, product perfection, design finesse, driving pleasure, etc. This is followed by an 'acceptor and rejecter' analysis, which takes into consideration customer feedback on what they think about a particular soon-to-be-launched car. In the last couple of years, as part of this leg of research, HMI has paid more attention to understanding customer behaviour in Tier II and Tier III cities. Finally, Hyundai takes feedback from industry experts and media on the prospects of the new launch.

All these efforts seem to be paying off handsomely. Today HMI's sales contribution to HMC is 14.4 per cent. HMI's market share in the passenger vehicles segment has grown from 18.20 per cent in 2012 to 21.90 in 2014 (till November). Indeed, the prolonged slump in the automobile industry did not stop the company from coming up with new offerings for the Indian market. In the last one year or so, HMI has launched four vehicles, namely, Xcent, Elite i20, Grand i10, and SantaFe. Of these, Grand i10 has been developed especially for the Indian market.

Back to Basics

That said, setting up with a sprawling research and development facility is not the only thing that will help a company get the most out of a market. To quote from the McKinsey article, 'To realise India's potential, multinationals must show a strong and visible commitment to the country, empower their local operations, and invest in local talent. They must pay closer attention to the needs of Indian consumers by offering the customisation in the local market as required'.

Nivea, which still sees itself as a challenger brand in India's Rs 3,400 crores skincare market, follows research practices borrowed from markets where the brand is a clear leader. It conducts regular user attitudinal studies across India to pick up valuable consumer insights. So far, Nivea has come up with around eight product innovations aimed particularly at the Indian market—these include Whitening Body Lotion, Men Dark Spot Reduction face wash, Men All In One face wash, and Total Face Cleanup, among others. In fact, Total Face Cleanup, launched last year, is testimony to how serious the company is about the Indian consumer. Research pointed out that in India, men and women in urban areas visit salons for facial clean-ups once a fortnight on an average. This set of people wash their faces two to three times a day with a face wash. Nivea's Total Face Cleanup is aimed to take care of the scrubbing needs of this target set in the interim period. Says Sunil Gadgil, marketing head, Nivea India, 'We are trying our best to customise our offerings for the Indian market. Going forward, we will leverage social media platforms to gain more consumer insights'.

Nivea, which doesn't have a manufacturing facility or an R&D centre in India at this point, is looking to set up its first R&D facility in Ahmedabad. Currently, all the products marketed in the country are imported from its manufacturing facilities located across Mexico, Germany, and Thailand. Market research inputs gathered from India are filtered in Dubai before manufacturing specs are laid down.

The onus laid on consumer research is even stronger if the company is operating in a category like food and beverages.

Around 1995, when McDonald's entered India, quick service restaurants (QSR) did not even exist as a category. Amit Jatia, owner, McDonald's India (West and South), recalls how focus groups were conducted around that time. Focus group participants then had no clue about the architecture of a burger or the concept of 'self-service'. At the most burgers were perceived as a snacking item, not as something that can be consumed at the time of lunch or dinner. Says Jatia, 'This perception has undergone a sea change since then. Over the next 10 years, as consumer confidence in the QSR format increased, more people walked in to try different items from our menu. We also introduced the burger to many new people by organising birthday parties and family gatherings at our outlets'.

The QSR chain realized early on that localization would be key in India. One of McDonald's early efforts in this area was the introduction of the hugely popular McAloo Tikki burger in 1997. This was followed by the development of the McPuff, Chicken McGrill, McVeggie, and most recently McPaneer Royale. Over the years, many of these local innovations have also been introduced in many new markets. McPuff, for instance, is now sold in West Asia, Aloo Tikki is sold in Singapore, and McVeggie in Malaysia and a few European markets.

The Latecomer is King

Ankur Bisen, senior vice-president, retail and consumer products at Technopak, says that over the last five years, there has been a steady increase in the number of pilots undertaken by multinationals and home-grown companies to get a complete picture of the Indian consumer. 'The main reason behind this is a change in the attitude of senior leadership of some of the leading organisations who now step out of their offices more often to bond with their Indian customers', says Bisen. Recently when Miami-based QSR chain Burger King launched its first outlet in Delhi, the company's entire leadership team including the CEO, CIO, CMO, and key investors, among others were seen managing queues and helping customers select food items from its menu.

While McDonald's took advantage of the lack of competition in its early years, Burger King entered India's Rs 5,500 crores (as of 2013) QSR category at a time when every third street-corner eatery proudly boasts of being the best burger-maker in town. To get its pre-launch homework spot-on, the company roped in global consulting firm McKinsey to conduct a comprehensive market assessment exercise.

The burger chain was pleasantly surprised to discover that India still has one of the lowest eat-out rates in the world with consumers stepping out only four times a month. In Singapore, a market not far removed from India, consumers eat out almost once every day. Burger King also found out that burger QSR chains account for only 2 per cent of the overall QSR pie in India, which is 17 per cent of the largely unorganized foods business.

Says Uma Talreja, chief marketing officer, Burger King India, 'Rather than focusing on how we can outdo the competition as part of our market research, we chose to invest in understanding what taste means for Indian consumers'.

A user attitude study was conducted in eight markets across the country by focusing on 35 groups of prospective customers. A common thread ran across all these groups: they like their burger spicy. At one level, this may seem obvious, but understanding what 'spicy food' means made the research worth every penny spent on it. For instance, spicy could mean hot or with loads of spices or a mix of both. Burger King's food scientists worked on these insights to come up with the right flavour. 'Today consumers can differentiate between what's cheap and what's value for money', adds Talreja.

Similar to the path followed by McDonald's, Pizza Hut, and Domino's in India, local innovation will be crucial to Burger King's expansion strategy in the country. For instance, Burger King's signature hamburger sandwich Whopper has been modified hereby replacing beef with lamb patty to suit the Indian palette. That apart, Chicken Tandoori Grill and King's Melt are two new items on the local menu. A group of food technologists, external chefs, and vendors came together to create the new recipes over a period of nine months. The final nod was given by the regional headquarters.

The next big challenge for Burger King is to see if customers who are sampling its entry-level burgers would try the other items on its menu. This will be done by following those who walk in with great loyalty programs and neat rewards—things that have stopped paying off in the Western markets but are just beginning to gain momentum back home.

Case Questions

1. What are the genetic and socio-economic issues which influence the buying behaviour of Indian customers?

2. The government policies of financial reforms as also the incentives for higher equity participation from foreign players in Indian businesses do not seem to have such an attraction for the foreign companies to get into the Indian market scenario compared to India's own domestic players. What really are the factors for such a situation?

15

Transforming the Asian Supply Chain

A Case Study in Supply Chain Management

Synopsis and Learning Objectives

Effective supply chain management helps businesses in the majority of situations calling for competitive advantage posturing for their products and services. Many businesses thrive on the strength of their supply chain capabilities in spite of severe competition and highly differentiated markets. Especially in the majority of Asian countries, it becomes difficult to exploit supply chain benefits due to the communication, connectivity, and commutation barricades and limitations.

The case study details how the protagonist company, Asian Steadfast Co. adapted unique systems and procedures to counter difficulties and succeed in otherwise hostile situations.

Case Details

Centralization of the Asian Supply Chain Organization

The objective for the Asian Supply Chain in the year 2000 was to save $30 million dollars over two to three years through supply chain rationalization. As a first step to ensure this objective was achieved, Steadfast centralized critical supply chain decisions at the new Asian headquarters in Beijing, China.

This approach created local management frustration and eventually resulted in a complete management turnaround in all of Steadfast's key Asian markets. There was a lot of organizational turbulence over a three-year period but a new management team was successfully put in place.

Indian Business Case Studies. Srilatha Palekar, Arun Pardhi and Sunanda Jindal, Oxford University Press. © ASM Group of Institutes, Pune, India 2022. DOI: 10.1093/oso/9780192869449.003.0015

Responsibility for overall supply chain planning was also transferred from the local (plant) level.

Previously local planning had been conducted using various Excel spreadsheets, which led to poor visibility of the business at the central level. As of 2003, three central planners conducted master planning per product category. They communicated on a day-by-day basis with the different production plants to ensure up-to-date information and coordination. Steadfast used a monthly master plan as a basis for production, but forecasts were updated on a weekly basis from actual sales figures.

Supply Chain Network Optimization

The most difficult challenge for Steadfast was to consolidate the national supply chains into a seamless Asian supply chain network in order to remain competitive. Uncompetitive factories in the Philippines and Indonesia were closed. The closures, combined with increased factory specialization, reduced the fixed administrative cost base, which had a positive impact on the company's bottom line.

In the short term, however, the decision was very costly for Steadfast. It negatively affected Steadfast Asia's 2001 profits, primarily because of the one-time cost of laying off 10% of the workforce. In addition to the optimization of the supply chain network, Steadfast further leveraged the production volume by insourcing previously outsourced production from subcontractors.

Product Standardization

Steadfast's strategy to grow through acquisitions in Asia had initially resulted in an unmanageable Asian brand portfolio. Since 2000 Steadfast Asia had viewed complexity reduction in its product portfolio as a key priority. Over the three-year period, the product portfolio was standardized primarily through harmonizing the product mix, an initiative that enabled the use of the same chemical ingredients to produce a large number of end-customer products and brands. For a large part of the product assortment, the main product differentiator was now the label and brand on the packaging, not the actual content of the product. This initiative put Steadfast in a position to reap the benefits from postponements, such as increased flexibility in production and supply chain planning.

Common IT Platform

Before 2000, the Asian supply chain network was not integrated through a common and transparent IT platform. Different IT solutions were used in each country, which made consolidation, reporting, and planning difficult. To address these inefficiencies, the decision was made to implement the SAP ERP system starting July 2000. However, unsatisfactory financial results in Asia made it necessary to postpone this twice. The implementation eventually started in 2002 and from the end of 2003, the SAP ERP system was up and running in all Asian factories. SAP was now the global IT platform, since business units in the US had been running on a common SAP ERP system for five years.

Leveraging Purchasing

Purchasing was identified as the 'low hanging fruit' in 2000. Steadfast's supplier base was highly fragmented. In combination with an uncoordinated purchasing approach throughout the supply chain network, purchasing became the key area to achieve quick savings. Analysis confirmed that Steadfast paid premium prices to suppliers, and that prices and contracts for the same products were significantly different at each plant. The response from Steadfast's management was to centralize sourcing globally in the United States. This strategy quickly paid off. The methods that were used to achieve savings were e-auctions, supplier rationalization, and complexity reduction by standardizing specifications.

Incentive Alignment

Steadfast's incentive system was primarily based on local performance. Performance appraisal and rewards were determined by the results achieved in a specific plant or market. As the supply chain focus changed from the local to the Asian level, the local incentive system was modified to include a global incentive package at the management level. Five global evaluation criteria were now used for all executives. In addition to the global measures, plant managers continued to be measured on plant performance. The transition to a global incentive approach was not easy. Steadfast was worried that it might lose its country focus, especially within the sales organization. Customers were mainly local and the sales organization was still very much locally based. Steadfast was also concerned that this shift could be perceived as a step towards removing the country manager position. To address these concerns, Steadfast continued to use country managers but added an Asian element of responsibility to the position (e.g. Asian responsibility for a given product category). Sales organizations also continued to be locally rewarded, at least at the level below manager.

Improving Customer Service

In 2000, Steadfast Asia had major issues with poor customer service levels. Key customers had threatened to leave if performance did not improve quickly. The cause was primarily a disconnected Asian supply chain and poor internal supply chain planning capabilities. Steadfast used the order fulfilment rate as the key performance indicator (KPI) to measure customer service levels. The order fulfilment rate subsequently improved to a level above 90% on average, primarily by increasing inventory levels.

The main important part of Steadfast's success is its supply chain management. Along with it SCM, there are obvious comprising factors such as just-in-time practices.

Steadfast has managed its logistics activities using the best possible way to drive down its costs and boost its sales which have led to an improvement of productivity and services. It was capable of shortening the pipeline by integrating its internal and external processes with employees, customers, and suppliers in order to keep minimum inventory stocks and to maximize its competitive advantage. Supply chain management takes into account the activities of all departments, especially the distribution one. Steadfast considered that storing, transporting, and distributing their products in an effective way, is very important. Its logistics played a major role in increasing the company's efficacy and in building the perfect picture among its competitors.

Supply chain management, then, is the active management of supply chain activities to maximize customer value and achieve a sustainable competitive advantage. It represents a conscious effort by the supply chain firms to develop and run supply chains in the most effective and efficient ways possible. Supply chain activities cover everything from product development, sourcing, production, and logistics, as well as the information systems needed to coordinate these activities.

The concept of supply chain management is based on two core ideas. The first is that practically every product that reaches an end-user represents the cumulative effort of multiple organizations. These organizations are referred to collectively as the supply chain.

The second idea is that while supply chains have existed for a long time, most organizations have only paid attention to what was happening within their 'four walls'. Few businesses understood, much less managed, the entire chain of activities that ultimately delivered products to the final customer. The result was disjointed and often ineffective supply chains.

The organizations that make up the supply chain are 'linked' together through physical flows and information flows. Physical flows involve the transformation, movement, and storage of goods and materials. They are the most visible piece of the supply chain. But just as important are information flows. Information flows allow the various supply chain partners to coordinate their long-term plans, and to control the day-to-day flow of goods and material up and down the supply chain.

Supply chain managers have a tremendous impact on the success of an organization. These managers are engaged in every facet of the business process—planning, purchasing, production, transportation, storage and distribution, customer service, and more! In short, these managers are the 'glue' that connects the different parts of the organization. Their performance helps organizations control expenses, boost sales, and maximize profits.

Two additional roles focus on facilitation and collaboration. Because supply chain managers touch so many different parts of the business, they are in a unique position to help other functions execute their strategies. They are also called upon to diagnose and support the needs of external supply chain partners. Here are just a few examples of these cross-functional roles:

- Effective selection and management of suppliers support lean manufacturing processes.
- Efficient transportation and distribution practices bolster marketing campaigns.
- Timely customer communication and technology-enabled visibility allow companies to monitor product flows and collaboratively respond to potential delivery problems.

Just-in-time means that just enough products are made to fulfil orders and limited stock is kept. Supplier involvement program was evolved to improve the product development efficiencies and effectiveness, which lead to development cost and reduction of developed time and reduce the cost and increase product value. Suppliers must install Just In Time (JIT), statistical operator control, and should work for continuous improvements. Supplier development must increase the performance and capability to meet the long-term supply need.

'Operational Excellence is the relentless drive to eliminate waste through daily, continuous, gradual improvement in everything we do, at all levels of the Company. In a similar way, continual improvement by dealers enables them to perform better and reach new customers with each passing day' (MINT News Paper).

Problems in the supply chain can hit businesses in many ways, the company noted. For instance, many businesses saw their brand reputation damaged earlier this year as a result of the horsemeat scandal, caused by insufficient oversight of trustworthy suppliers.

When it comes to managing supply chains, the people in charge have several issues to deal with. Each issue facing your supply chain manager has implications for your company—including its bottom line and its customers—so it's important to keep these issues in mind when developing and analysing your supply chain.

Current supply chains are growing in complexity due to several factors. We, the customers, are demanding innovative products at the right time and at a reasonable price. This creates challenges for companies since creating both responsive and cost-effective supply chains is critically difficult. Let me expand on today's main supply chain challenges.

- Globalization
- Customer preferences
- Market growth
- Managing suppliers
- Maintaining safety and quality
- Shorter lead time, less inventory, and better throughput
- Access to latest technology

The Insights

The five issues cited by The Chief Supply Chain Officer Report 2013 were:

1. The need to continue to reduce costs while improving customer service and supporting expansion in new markets and product lines. Some 68 per cent of respondents said operating cost reduction is 'very important compared with 64 per cent in 2011' (MINT News Paper).

2. The need to manage the 'complexity of "omnichannel or Multichannel retailing" selling and customer fulfilment'. More than half (55 per cent) said the demands of e-commerce and mobile-enabled consumers are increasing the number of stock-keeping units they have to support. Almost 55 per cent reported they are building new distribution centres, and 48 per cent are building direct-to-customer fulfilment capabilities.

3. The fact boards expect lower costs and greater efficiency. Nearly half (47 per cent) agreed this was the case this year, up from 43 per cent last year, and 32 per cent in 2011.

4. Following the horsemeat scandal, safety and quality incidents are at the top of the risk index, with 37 per cent reporting that they are 'very concerned' about this for 2013–2014 and 35 per cent are 'concerned'.

5. Facilitating career progression, developing new production skills and demonstrating a return on investment is a further issue.

Three-quarters (76 per cent) said providing compelling career options for talented supply chain staff is 'challenging', this is up from 66 per cent in each of the previous two years. Some 53 per cent believe new product introduction and launch capabilities are now 'essential' for the supply chain, up from just 18 per cent in 2011. And 53 per cent of respondents—and 31 per cent of those spending 5 per cent or more of their personnel costs on training and development—say they don't track return on investment.

Case Questions

1. Narrate your observations from the case study as to what stands out as a unique practice in the supply chain management activities of Steadfast Asia Co. and whether you agree that in todays' difficult time, such a system could succeed?

2. With global upheavals due mainly to ongoing trade wars between major nations in the world, the main victim has been the supply chain management with major sources shifting alliances and protectionism under the garb of national interests businesses are suffering on account of supply-side shortages. How do you think the aspirations of global supply chains could be sustained under uncertain trade restrictions?

16

Can Toyota Regain Its Footing in India?

A Case Study on Product Positioning and Turnaround Strategy

Learning Objectives

The intricacies and complexity of the Indian automobile sector are not new to any domestic or global automobile company. Many have tried their luck over the previous two decades but no one has been able to make any meaningful success story in the Indian auto segment.

Toyota entered India with its Qualis brand of SUVs in the early 2000s, followed by successive model introduction in the hatchback car segment like the Etios right up its creamy brands like Innova and many more, stopping short of its luxury brands.

As is the case with many foreign brands such as GM, Fiat, Ford, Honda, Toyota is stuck in sluggish market prospects and its entry brand Qualis has been grounded due to quality issues.

The real issues are peculiar with the Indian automobile market, wherein it is very difficult for a global brand to break through the Indian customer psyche of sensitivity to product pricing and long-term durability issues.

For students in marketing focusing on product pricing and positioning, this case study offers interesting insights.

Synopsis

From localization to cost control measures to small hybrid cars, Toyota is pulling out all stops in its recovery bid. For Toyota's Indian operations, small isn't beautiful; it is unprofitable. At least, that's what the numbers

Indian Business Case Studies. Srilatha Palekar, Arun Pardhi and Sunanda Jindal, Oxford University Press. © ASM Group of Institutes, Pune, India 2022. DOI: 10.1093/oso/9780192869449.003.0016

would appear to suggest. Toyota Kirloskar Motor Pvt. Ltd incurred a loss of Rs 180 crores in the fiscal year ended 31 March 2014, marking a dubious first in the Japanese automaker's 15-year history in India. The loss was largely on account of a recent focus on the small-car Liva and the entry-level sedan Etios for a company that has always made money in India on the back of a focus on workhorse-like utility vehicles—the iconic Qualis first, and then the Innova—and up-market sedans such as the popular Corolla.

The launches were part of Toyota's effort to play the volumes game in India based on its understanding of where the market was headed: 10 million passenger vehicle market by 2025—five times its current size—prompting a push for alternative strategies and newer models. Only Toyota's bet on economies of scale from the Etios brand to drive profits came a cropper due to a lack of consumer interest.

It was caught on the wrong foot because its localization efforts were not at par with the industries. It didn't seem to understand the Indian customer. And it seemed to have forgotten the famed Toyota way that emphasizes cost and quality.

Vikram Kirloskar, the vice-chairman of the Indian unit, agrees. 'In hindsight, everything that we did seems wrong,' he said in an interview earlier this month. 'Why haven't Etios and Liva taken off if they are so good in terms of performance?' 'Toyota's only pain points in India are Liva and Etios,' said Gurgaon-based Deepesh Rathore, co-founder and director at Emerging Market Automotive Advisory (Emaa).

According to Rathore, the cars are a mismatch of expectations—both for the company, which was not used to making a low-cost car but forced itself into it and struggled to meet the price target, and for the customers who did not find the models living up to quality and aspirations. Sales of the Liva declined 20 per cent during the last fiscal and 13.27 per cent in the five months to August this fiscal year. Sales of the Etios sedan declined 19.44 per cent and 15.5 per cent during the same periods, respectively.

The Case Details

Toyota decided to change lanes, and the new direction came from the top, with a revamp of the leadership. On 31 January 2015, Toyota announced top-level management changes in its Indian arm. Sandeep Singh, deputy managing director (sales, marketing, customer service, and commercial divisions) was moved to a new role in its Asia-Pacific operations. N. Raja, senior vice-president, and Akitoshi Takemura, senior managing coordinator, took joint responsibility for sales and marketing. T.S. Jaishankar, executive vice-president and director, was given charge of commercial functions, and Hitoshi Iwanaga, senior vice-president, took charge of customer services.

In a move underscoring the importance of India in Toyota's global scheme, in January 2014, Toyota Motor Corp. deputed Naomi Ishii, a 24-year veteran at the Japanese manufacturer who was general manager of the strategic planning department in Japan, as managing director, Toyota India. He comes with a clear mandate from the headquarters—rapid localization of models and understanding the big challenges posed by the small-car market in India. 'Toyoda san (president and chief executive officer of Toyota Motor Corp., Akio Toyoda) has sent his best man to head the India operations. That shows the significance of the Indian unit', Kirloskar said.

The Toyota way, a shrinking car market (India's passenger car market shrank for the first time in 11 years in 2013–2014), high fuel prices and a weak rupee further singed the company's earnings. On 28 August 2013, the Indian rupee plunged to an all-time low of 68.85 against the dollar, sending alarm bells ringing at the Bangalore-headquartered firm that was already under pressure due to shrinking volumes.

The high reliance on imported parts meant the company's import bill would soar. It was time to aggressively pursue a strategy it hadn't paid much attention to so far—localization. Compared to their existing models, the two new models introduced by Toyota had higher local content at the time of their launch. That wasn't enough. At the time of the launch, the local content in both the cars was 70 per cent, whereas rivals such as Maruti Suzuki India Ltd and Hyundai Motor India Ltd have cars in this segment with nearly 90 per cent local content. Over the years, Toyota too has increased local content with the commencement of local production of engines and transmission units. It is up to 90 per cent for petrol models now, according to the company's spokesperson.

It was also time for Toyota to implement what it has been teaching, and the world has been immensely benefiting from—the Toyota Production

System, a management philosophy based on the core principles of elimination of waste (muda), inconsistency (mura), and overburden (muri). 'Even a Rs.1 reduction is seen as a major initiative in Toyota', Kirloskar said.

Over the last one-and-a-half years, more than the drop in volumes, it was cost inflation—a sign of excess flab in the system—that worried the management. Now, what began as a small initiative—to switch off the lights when not needed—has morphed into a major cost-pruning exercise across business functions. 'We brought everyone and everything together so that everyone's ideas can be implemented, making it very clear it's not only a management issue. This is the Toyota Production System in its true sense', said Kirloskar.

From changing the mix of models and reducing friction in machines to improving the yield from the steel and other raw materials to doing away with discounts on models and salary hikes for those above the level of deputy general manager, the company is sharply focusing on costs. It is hoping to make a small profit by end of the current fiscal year, said Shekar Viswanathan, vice-chairman at the firm.

With the changes in the internal cost structure, Toyota has, according to Kirloskar, managed to reduce the break-even volumes at its plant to 125,000–150,000 units per annum, half its installed capacity. It has also reduced its operating costs by 15 per cent to 20 per cent.

Declining sales during the last fiscal year, Toyota's overall sales in the passenger vehicle market declined 22 per cent to 56,865 units and its market share dropped to 5.14 per cent from 6.21 per cent a year ago, according to the Society of Indian Automobile Manufacturers (SIAM).

But on back of the economic recovery, the car market has now shown some early signs of revival, with sales rising 4.5 per cent in the five months to August. Toyota's efforts too seem to be paying off, with sales rising 2 per cent to 54,539 in the same period—albeit on a low base. 'The overall numbers may not be looking impressive, but we have no inventory and we are running pillar to post to meet demand; we have waiting lists everywhere as we had curtailed production to align ourselves to the slow market', Kirloskar said. 'For us, the most important thing is that we are seeing black numbers every month since the last four months with whatever volumes we are producing'.

To be sure, the unsuccessful bid to introduce models in the mass seg-ment has slowed the company's progress and forced it to recalibrate its strategy, said an industry expert. 'It had a lot riding on the Etios and Liva, the models developed ground-up for India. A bleak sales response slowed the company's future product strategy', said Rakesh Batra, partner and national leader, automotive practice, at audit and consulting firm EY.

In a market where new models have become an imperative for survival, mere refreshes do not work, he added. The Etios and the Liva have hurt Toyota's brand image in the country, Ishii said in an interview, adding that the company has checked the damage control and is happy with the cur-rent sales volumes in the segment.

Yet, the company would not have been able to work on its strategy of becoming an important player in India's car market without launching a small car. Small cars account for seven of every 10 cars sold in India. Indeed, the lack of models may have also resulted in Toyota ceding market share to rivals.

An intensely competitive market has seen a spate of model launches by rivals including Honda Cars India Ltd, Hyundai Motor India, and Maruti Suzuki. But Toyota has been conspicuous by its absence in so-called com-pact sports utility vehicles (SUVs) and the compact sedan.

The company hasn't introduced any new model since the launch of the Etios and the Liva in 2010, although it has launched variants and exten-sions such as the Etios Cross, a cross-over based on the Etios platform.

It may take some more time before the company introduces a new model, Ishii said. 'We are in an intense discussion regarding the mid- and long-term product line-up and business planning for India by redefining our position with the stakeholders in our headquarters. Accordingly, we can find out what we have to start', Ishii said.

In his initial study, Ishii has identified the so-called B-segment (com-pact cars) as a priority. He is in the process of submitting a detailed report to Toyota headquarters, and a final decision regarding the product line-up for India should be taken in a year.

Till then, increasing sales in the compact segment will be the company's top priority, he added. As for small cars, he added, 'we have adjusted our expectations. This is not necessarily the objective that we set up in the be-ginning of the operation'. And as the company works even towards those adjusted numbers, it is hoping to understand Indian car buyers better. India's diverse profile of car buyers, according to Ishii has been a challenge, especially for a company used to the homogeneity of Japan.

Tax conundrum, a unique market character that is heavily driven by the taxation system, is another reason Toyota's sales have been slow, he said, citing the sub-4m small-car segment that has spawned a new body type in India. Cars with a length lower than 4m are taxed less. 'No other country has such a segment', he said.

Toyota is not the only firm that has found it tough to respond to the emergence of new body types such as the compact sedan and SUVs—a concept that is unique to India. Others, too, are struggling to come up with models and at the right price. 'We realized that we can't transplant European cost structures here', Mahesh Kodumudi, president and managing director at Volkswagen India Pvt. Ltd, said in an interview in February, adding that 'India is one of the most challenging markets in the VW (Volkswagen) world'.

Honda India, which too was struggling till March 2013, managed to revive its India fortunes with the launch of the Amaze compact sedan last year. Ishii also wants to introduce hybrid models in India, a field in which Toyota is very strong. The company sells hybrids of some larger models in the country but wants to introduce small hybrid cars, too. 'We really want to promote hybridization. Right now, we have the Camry hybrid. Even though the sales numbers are really small, they are picking up. We need to introduce some small models in this area', he said.

Case Questions

1. Toyota came into India as a part of economic reforms and encouragement and incentives for foreign direct investments, more so in the automobile industry. Initially, Toyota, in a strategic alliance with Kirloskars, brought in models such as Qualis, which were workhorses in their own regime and responsible for Toyotas Volume growths in global markets. But soon, due mainly to pollution control regulations and stricter road safety concerns, Toyota faced a major setback and had to withdraw its entry-level products. Was this a clever strategy for a company like Toyota with global repute

to enter the Indian market with older technology products and face humiliating rejections from customers and regulatory authorities in India?

2. Toyota Kirloskar is embroiled in eternal IR issues as an effect of its management's inept handling of IR and ER issues prompted by the loss of market and customer preference to its products in India. Will Toyota roll back its sleeves for rejuvenation in its product portfolio or it's a swan song for Toyota in India?

17

The Shining 'Soblin' in Limelight

A Case Study on a Budding Business in Medical Products in Mexico

Learning Objectives

Many entrepreneurs in emerging economies like Mexico are finding it as a major challenge to enter markets, calling for product innovation at the snap of an eyelid. This is more pronounced in countries that have been heavily dependent on imports rather than domestic manufacture of goods and services in the medical electronics and robotic equipment needed for innovation and new product development.

This case study is of a promising medium-scale industry in Western Mexico trying its best by developing medical prosthetic arms manufacture as a substitute for the huge imports made from the United States. The entrepreneurial zeal to succeed and the enormous issues to face are positioned juxtopposing to each other for successful way forward.

For students in entrepreneurship development, the case study will definitely be of much use in understanding the fundamental characteristics of a capable enterprise with a clear vision, mission, and strategic objectives.

Synopsis

It is a business devoted to the sale and globalized distribution of medical products: bionic ankle-foot prostheses and knee prostheses, as well as providing technological and innovative services of the highest quality, offered at a competitive price.

Indian Business Case Studies. Srilatha Palekar, Arun Pardhi and Sunanda Jindal, Oxford University Press. © ASM Group of Institutes, Pune, India 2022. DOI: 10.1093/oso/9780192869449.003.0017

One of the main drivers of this product development is the opportunity to market the second bionic foot and knee prosthesis worldwide and to be the first company in Latin America to market bionic prostheses for people with transtibial amputation and/or transfemoral.

At present, there are only less than ten companies worldwide that sell bionic prostheses, referring to prostheses of all kinds, from bionic eyes to bionic legs.

Case Details

According to the World Health Organization, it is estimated that 10 per cent of the world's adult population has diabetes. Globally there are approximately 415 million people who suffer from this disease and in Mexico alone, it is estimated that there are 11 million people with diabetes. The prevalence of diabetes has increased more rapidly in recent years and is expected to continue to increase as a result of the increase in adults worldwide. Diabetics are the most susceptible to amputation. Between 40 per cent and 85 per cent of lower extremity amputations are related to diabetes. Lower limb amputations are the most prevalent. In Mexico in 2012, 27,375 amputations were practiced and in the United States, an average of 185,000 amputations were practiced annually. It is estimated that by 2050 the number of people with amputation will increase to 200 per cent.

The use of foot and/or knee prostheses is a common practice in amputees of the lower limbs in order to be able to move from one place to another. It is evident that there is a wide market for the manufacture of bionic prostheses, these in turn favour to increase the quality of life of the people with the efficiency, quality, and high technology of the products.

Global Medical Bionic Implants Market

Bionics involves the study of biological systems in order to develop artificial systems that can replicate their functions. Bionic implants are mechanical or electronic systems that function like living organisms or parts of living organisms. Bionics, when extended to the field of medicine, seeks to replace or enhance organs or parts of the human body using artificial prosthesis. The market is expected to grow at a Cumulative Average Growth Rate (CAGR) of 7.1 per cent from 2012 to 2017 to reach $17.82 billion by 2017.

For purposes of this document, non-invasive prostheses or also known as external prostheses, will be classified into three classes: passive prostheses, semi-passive prostheses, active prostheses, or also known as bionic prostheses. Following the same order of classification of prosthetic devices, passive prostheses are the most rudimentary and the bionic prostheses are the most technological.

The passive prostheses are the ones of greater use, to be of easy access and to be those of lower cost. The cost of a prosthesis of this classification walks in an average of 14,000 pesos. Unlike passive prostheses, semi-passive prostheses are more functional and ergonomic and therefore their price is even greater. The price of semi-passive prostheses is maintained at a price of around 275,000 pesos.

Both prostheses have something in common, and they do not restore the functionality of the member they are replacing. People who use prosthetics of this classification tend to walk up to 50 per cent slower and to fatigue up to 70 per cent more compared to a person with their healthy limbs. If it were not enough, passive and semi-passive prostheses cause joint pain, provide asymmetrical walking, and increase the risk of surgical operation for spinal damage.

Artificial Organs and Bionic Implants

Currently, the global market is dominated by North America, primarily due to higher per capita income and increased awareness among the population. Following North America are Europe and Asia-Pacific. The Latin American market is filled with potential and is penetrated only to a certain extent. This is due to the increased awareness among the population. There is great scope for new entrants in the emerging markets of Asia and Latin America.

Some of the factors contributing to the growth of the market are:

- Rapidly aging population
- Increased number of people suffering from organ failures
- Rising incidents of motor accidents and injuries

- Rapid technological advancements in the bionics sector
- Huge scarcity of donor organs for organ transplantations

Some of the factors limiting the growth of the market are:

- Stringent regulatory framework for the use of artificial organs and bionics
- Fear of malfunction or failure of device
- Huge criticism from a sector of healthcare professionals

The market is segmented by type and technology. By type, the market is segmented into artificial heart, kidney, liver, pancreas and lungs, and cochlear, vision, orthopaedic and brain bionics, and exoskeletons. By technology, the market is segmented into electrical and mechanical.

What Is Soblin?

Soblin, a company that will be founded by our work team in order to offer innovative and high-quality products in the area of bionics. The company intends to bring to market the first bionic knee prosthesis worldwide and the second bionic prosthesis standing worldwide. Compared to BIONX our product will be offered at an affordable price, up to seven times lower. Soblin is targeting a socio-economic sector that BIONX has not been able to cover due to the price of its product. Our products and services will be offered at competitive prices and credit and payment facilities will be granted to the customer.

The products will be sold directly to the patient, technicians in prosthetics, companies, hospitals, clinics, and private and governmental institutions of the health sector. It is worth mentioning that our main clients will be insurance companies and government institutions.

Under the direction, the project of the active prosthesis in the laboratories and classrooms of the Faculty of Engineering of the Autonomous University of Baja California. With more than five years of scientific research and development, the results of the technological advances of the prosthesis have been published in scientific journals and presented in national and international congresses, mentioning countries such as

France and Colombia. Due to the dedication and experience acquired in the field of biomedical engineering in parallel to this project in 2014, the Technological Rehabilitation Institute, also known by its acronym ITR, emerges. ITR is a research and development centre for medical devices and rehabilitation. This institute is developing the project of the bionic prosthesis.

Business Model

Offer our products and services at competitive prices and with payment facilities to companies, hospitals, rehabilitation clinics, private and governmental institutions, and individuals.

Mission: Provide world-class products and services that benefit the health and quality of life of people with lower limb amputation.

Vision: To be a leading company and of national and international prestige in the generation of products and services of the highest quality in the field of bionic engineering.

Goals

1. To guarantee the fulfilment of the services granted to customers and ensure full satisfaction.
2. To meet the needs of the market with social responsibility.
3. To develop innovative products that adapt to the diversity of people and their affections.
4. To generate products and services according to the needs, requirements, and expectations of customers.
5. To acquire the necessary knowledge and tools to implement and maintain a management system of quality in medical products.

Values

1. Responsibility: We are responsible and in solidarity with society, the environment, our collaborators, customers, and consumers.

2. Passion: We deliver with passion in everything we do to be a leader in the market.
3. Teamwork: We work as a team and join efforts to achieve great achievements.
4. Innovation: We promote new ideas oriented to the efficiency and satisfaction of our customers and consumers.
5. Quality: Our greatest commitment to the customer is to offer the best service and superior quality products.

Competitive Advantage

The prosthetic products of inferior members that are available in the national market are completely mechanical and passive. These devices fail to restore the basic function of the member being replaced, and they do not have sufficient elements to provide the necessary support for the person to perform his normal daily activities.

The prostheses that Soblin is developing and will offer to the national and international market are active types.

Unlike passive prostheses, their prostheses feature actuators, sensors, and microcomputers that together make up a system that provides the functionality and support that a lower limb or leg naturally provides.

The advantages of these products and equipment compared to others in the market lie in the technology used, the use of unconventional methods for the manufacture of the product and the quality of work. Competitive prices will also be offered that will be of high impact for consumers.

Organizational Structure of Soblin

President

Responsible for the coordination and implementation of new product development programs in the medical device industry. Manage and develop multiple research and development projects for the innovation and improvement of current medical devices, such as bionic prostheses of lower limbs, low-cost passive prostheses, orthoses, and robotic rehabilitation equipment. Creation of work plans for the implementation of research activities. Responsible for linking and creating collaboration agreements with governmental and private institutions, such as the management and delegation of the projects resulting therefrom.

Engineering Research and Development

Management of research projects and development of medical devices. Design, development, and manufacture of peripheral catheters (PICC), haemodialysis catheters, implantable ports,, introducers, and production tools. Incharge of the automation of production lines and the creation of new tools is responsible to facilitate the manufacture, profitability, and reduce costs of production and the final product.

Production Planning

Responsible for controlling and planning everything in the area of production, logistic of materials, supplies, machinery, or other required plans and organizes the actions to be followed before a certain project and directs the personnel to comply with standards established by the management, coordinates, analyses, supports, and implements organized and methodical work plans that will allow more and better results in the shortest possible time.

Production Supervisor

He is responsible for managing, directing, coordinating, the processes of production of products or raw material that will be used to meet market demand, is also basically a supervisor of production processes according to stipulated quality standards.

Quality Supervisor

Verifies the total quality of the product or service and for this count on the same human resource, material, and equipment necessary for the assurance of the same, handles a list of suppliers and looks for the best product offers, seeks to optimize resources effectively by verifying that all department standards are being met in terms of measurements of overall quality of products along with productivity and adherence to delivery schedules.

Chief Sales Officer

Its main function is to implement sales plans that are aligned with the goals and vision of strategic planning; if your company owns several vendors, it is the responsibility of the CSO to motivate them, guide them and train them so that their sales team reaches its goal.

Conclusions

Soblin Company has a clear strategy for the future of the development of active and passive bionic prostheses that will revolutionize the current market, taking advantage of current competitive advantages and creating technological innovations that guarantee the permanence of the business in the future. Currently, it is working with several universities and centres of research in Baja California. Being the most representative of the State to enter the strategic projects of the company, such as the Santander Award for Business Innovation–Fondo Francisco Gallego Monge Award, of which the company was the beneficiary of the first place as the campaigns with groups of civil society for the day of passive research to vulnerable communities in Baja California through the foundation supported by the Technological Institute of Rehabilitation of the TIR, with these actions Soblin seeks to consolidate itself as the first company in the northwest region of Mexico to create these products of high impact with a vision of the future regarding the international level in the biomedical sector, achieving sustainability and economic development.

Case Questions

1. What are the success factors to ensure the sustainable growth of Soblin?

2. Does the company have a vision and clear strategic objectives aligned with the mission of the company?

3. What is the competitive advantage of the company and how can it profit most from it? This advantage directly depends on the core business of the company.

4. What is the analysis of the environment? What strategies are appropriate for the company to reach its maximum potential?

18

Ford, Can It Afford?

Ford Motors Ltd—Long Search for Profits in Emerging Markets

Learning Objectives

Understanding Indian customer behaviour and customer experience have ever been an interesting topic and task for many global business entities who, after having been in India for decades, are not clear
of the customer expectations and behaviour so peculiar to the Indian
sub-continent, especially with thousands of castes and cultural inhibitions which make it extremely difficult for someone who has been otherwise successful elsewhere finds it difficult to succeed equally in Indian
markets.

The automobile giants of the world, you may name anyone who has invested in India with high hopes on capturing a major market share, have
not been able to exceed 5 per cent of the huge automobile market in India.

Ford Motors is one among the pioneering world-class automotive
group to enter the Indian automotive markets, which over two decades
has been trying its level best to even breakeven, leave alone any meaningful position at Indian automobile market share.

Synopsis

Many global stalwarts in the automotive industry have found it difficult to establish market dominance in emerging markets like India in
spite of decades of focused attention in understanding such markets
and investing heavily to offer technologically advanced products and

Indian Business Case Studies. Srilatha Palekar, Arun Pardhi and Sunanda Jindal, Oxford University Press. © ASM
Group of Institutes, Pune, India 2022. DOI: 10.1093/oso/9780192869449.003.0018

after-sales for their products. It is even today a pathetic situation that such global wizards find it difficult to sustain and survive in emerging markets. This case study attempts to highlight a few such efforts by Ford Motor Company which entered the Indian market in the early 90s but as on today stuck in deteriorating market share and not many Indian strategic partners too to help ease out the situation for Ford in India.

Late last year, when Ford Motor Company CEO Alan Mulally offered David Schoch, Ford's Asia Pacific former CFO (currently president, Asia Pacific), the top job in the region, Schoch had just one question for his boss: 'Are we committed to the region... from Bill Ford to all the way down. Alan said yes. And I said yes (to the job)', recalls Schoch.

His question resonates in Ford's India context too, but in a slightly different way. Ford first started selling cars here in 1996. Since then, six CEOs have led Ford India, which has sunk in $2 billion in investments and launched nine models. Seventeen years later, all that Ford has to show in India is a market share of less than 3 per cent, a plant that was working at half its capacity (2012–2013) and Rs 1,374 crores in accumulated losses.

'Earlier, Ford wasn't focused on India', Mulally, chairman, Ford Motors, recently admitted to a group of Indian journalists in Chennai. 'We were number one in the US, launching vehicles in Europe. But we took the big decision six years ago that we wanted to grow in every part of the world, and we were willing to commit investments', said Mulally. Since then, Ford has sharpened its India focus, developed new platforms and products, in the process of building a new plant in Sanand, Gujarat, which will double capacity.

The 'are you committed to India' question is no longer asked of Ford. But now, Ford is facing a return-on-investment question. If it can't make profits 17 years after setting shop in India, when will it? 'We are running a marathon... we are continuing to invest', says Joginder Singh, president and MD of Ford India. To be fair, Ford reported a cash profit of Rs 144 crores in FY12. But a depreciation charge of Rs 284 crores pushed it to losses. Many industry analysts say it's about time Ford shows hard profits in India. 'To say that the company has been making huge investments is an excuse for non-performance on profits', says BVR Subbu, an industry veteran who has worked many years in Tata Motors and Hyundai.

The same is the case with the other US auto major, General Motors (GM), which has accumulated Rs 746 crores in losses in 18 years. But it is not as if MNC car makers haven't made money in India. Hyundai, the only MNC Korean carmaker with sizeable exports and higher indigenization, saw profits grow from Rs 376 crores in fiscal 2010 to Rs 830 crores two years later and is threatening the Numero Uno Position of Maruti Suzuki in the compact car segment.

CEO Continuity

A Ford India CEO, on an average, stays at the helm for less than three years. That may also be one part of the profitability problem, industry watchers say. Lack of continuity in the leadership does impact the long-term perspective and performance of the company.

Ford disagrees. 'We are a huge family, part of the One Ford academy and veterans with the company', says Singh. 'We are trained under one global platform. The strategy remains the same. We stay the course and are resilient'.

Adds VinayPiparsania, ED, marketing, sales, and service: 'There might be leadership changes, but the overall strategy does not change frequently. There is continuity among functional heads. The MD or the CEO is supported by the operating committee, which does not change frequently in its entirety'.

Typically, large multinational corporations have a continuity strategy in place for CEO positions, says Aditya Narayan Mishra, president, Randstad India. Too many changes at the top level can lead to temporary disruptions. It is felt that a CEO should stay around in a company for seven years to feel the real impact of the position, Mishra adds.

Ultimately, It's About the Cars

To some extent at least, Ford India's CEO changes mirrors the company's start-stop-start progress in the country. Ford hit the bull's-eye with its small car Figo, which was launched by former CEO Michael Boneham in 2010. Its attractive pricing worked initially, but it failed to sustain the momentum two years into the launch. Even an upgrade in 2012 did not excite the market. (Even though on JD Power rating, it won the Best Car Award for two years in succession.)

Before that, the Ikon rolled out under another former CEO, Philip G. Spender, also did well soon after its launch, but this too fizzled out after a while. Ford India has often struggled with a long gap between two successful models.

In mid-2010, riding on the success of Figo and realizing India's strategic importance, Ford announced plans to launch eight new models by 2015. Only two models—Fiesta and EcoSport—have rolled out till now. Fiesta failed to enthuse buyers and a lot is riding on the EcoSport, launched last month. 'Ford has not only been juggling with many models, but its products are (also) not exciting enough', says Subbu. 'It has never been able to compete with Hyundai on pricing. While the Ikon started as a segment leader, it slipped in numbers to the Hyundai Accent'.

Subbu says, 'To turn profitable, a (car) company needs to obtain a minimum volume of a specific model. For models in the Rs 5–7.5 lakh range, a company needs to sell at least 3,000 units a month to break even, and 6,000 units a month for products in the Rs 3–5 lakh price range'.

Adds Mahantesh Sabarad, senior VP-Equity Research, Fortune Equity Brokers, says, 'Ford cannot rely on a single model success story'.

'The recent launches—Figo and EcoSport—appear to be in line with the need of the Indian customer', says Jagdish Khattar, ex-MD of Maruti Suzuki and current MD of Carnation India. '(But) the need to meet customers' post-sale requirements, where expectations are high, will remain and need to be met'.

'For a sustainable market share, the company needs to break into the 5 per cent plus market share category, which effectively means being in the top 5 of the Indian car market', adds Sabarad. 'The key is to increase volumes, distribution reach, brand visibility and launch volume-pullers'.

For the drive ahead, Ford will need to induct newer models in new segments to have a well-rounded portfolio and increase localization to bring down cost and sell overseas. The Figo hatchback brought the company back into the reckoning and India will be a key exports hub for 'EcoSport', which will be shipped to over 40 countries, including Europe, Australia, South Africa, and Taiwan (Ford has registered an opening booking of 30,000 numbers for its EcoSports as per reports).

How Exports Can Help P&L

Ford's manufacturing capacity in Chennai is 200,000 vehicles and 340,000 engines. Only about 54 per cent of this was utilized in FY-13. Once Sanand gets operational, Ford's annual capacity in India will be 440,000 vehicles and 610,000 engines per annum. It will need more than a few high-volume and highly successful models if it has to squeeze returns out of this huge capacity. It will also need exports.

Sources close to the company say utilization of India's cost-effective manufacturing base as a hub to export B-segment cars and smaller engines will help Ford India break into profits. Hyundai's path to profitability, for example, was accelerated by exports.

Ford is also developing a new compact car platform, code named 'B562', which may become the base for three new models, four people close to the development told ET. The plan is to produce 220,000–240,000 units of the B562 platform in the first year, out of which 50,000–60,000 units will be exported. The overseas shipment will eventually increase to 120,000–140,000 units per annum as the company adds new markets.

It also learnt that Ford would export 35,000 units of EcoSport, making up for almost 33 per cent of its total production plan of 109,000 units in 2014. All this could step up capacity utilization and cover fixed costs better.

'A big export push will help Ford not only in getting the pricing right for the domestic market a la EcoSport, but also make available some of the high-end technology at an affordable price', says VG Ramakrishnan, MD, Frost & Sullivan, South Asia. 'With the stringent implementation of transfer pricing, Ford's Indian operation will be exporting vehicles for a decent profit. With higher exports, the balance sheet will get a boost and the company can recoup losses faster', he adds.

The company is aiming to export 35 to 50 per cent of the total production and achieve optimum plant utilization to reduce cost per car. Ford India can make faster returns by running its plant around the clock.

Tom Chackalackal, ED at Ford India, in a recent interview, said the focus is on sweating existing assets. 'Everyone globally under the One Ford umbrella is trying to see how we can fill Chennai the fastest and pump out volumes', adds Chackalackal. That's a simple enough prescription—make, sell, and export more cars. That's bound to bring in the profits. Only, Ford is still figuring out how 17 years after it set foot in India.

Case Questions

1. Tracing the journey of Ford Motors in India over nearly two decades, it has not been able to even achieve a breakeven level on its investments made so far. Do you feel the introduction of new models and wishful planning on exports to have exponential growth is the right strategy for Ford in emerging markets like India?

2. There are comments on Ford's frequent changes at the CEO levels in Indian operations. Do you think this is an important impediment for consolidations at the marketplace for Ford products in India?

3. With all global giants vying for a reasonable share in the pie of the Indian passenger car segment (even cross-over models such as Duster by Nissan, other competing brands of Volkswagen, and many more), will Ford be able to realize its strategic intents of turn around in the car segment?

19
Biyani vs. Ambani

A Case Study on the E-commerce Tussle

Learning Objectives

To evaluate various opportunities on an ongoing basis. Trying to figure out the Indian consumer and crack the retail code. The industrial mindset to focus on logistics, distribution, and supply chain helped.

Synopsis

In any new sector, be it airline, telecom, or retail, one pioneer gives it a start and it is up to the second business to take it to the next level. The belief is that, as in most global markets, a homegrown retailer will set the marker in India and Reliance wants to be that homegrown retailer. RIL is not looking at taking a pie of the existing market and is focused on growing the market.

Case Details

It's no comparison, Kishore Biyani says calmly down a phone line, about a storyline that seeks to compare his business, personality, and operating style with that of an industry captain who might be his nearest competitor in the retail business, but whose main business generates more in profits than Biyani's does in revenues.

Out of reverence for Mukesh Ambani and rare reticence on his own part, Biyani declines to speak for this story. But the storyline—Biyani

Indian Business Case Studies. Srilatha Palekar, Arun Pardhi and Sunanda Jindal, Oxford University Press. © ASM Group of Institutes, Pune, India 2022. DOI: 10.1093/oso/9780192869449.003.0019

versus Ambani; Future Group versus Reliance Retail—won't go away. If anything, it has acquired an immediacy that is all the more compelling for the contrasts it throws up.

There are Reliance Retail's latest financial results. Announced last week as part of the results of its parent, Reliance Industries Limited (RIL), those numbers show that, in terms of annual turnover, Reliance Retail has crossed Rs 10,000 crores and is breathing down Future Group's neck, which had a nine-year head start. From Rs 4,271 crores in 2010, the gap in revenues has closed to, analysts estimate, about Rs 2,000 crores.

Another year and Reliance might inch ahead. There are people's movements. A handful of trusty, senior Biyani aides have changed sides, notably Sanjay Jog and Damodar Mall, and this has caused some consternation to a man who is known to wear his heart on his sleeve even when running a Rs 12,000-crore retail empire. 'We always have an emotional relationship with our employees. So, it can be difficult during parting', Biyani had told ET last month during an interaction for another story.

And there are the contrasts. Both businesses stand at pivotal—and strikingly contrasting—points in their respective journeys. While Future resembles a bird whose wings have been clipped, Reliance is taking flight. While Future is in rebuilding mode, Reliance is taking its building to another level. While Biyani is returning from a 'vanvas' (exile) to play a larger role in Future, Ambani, who too declined to speak for this story, is a distant presence in Reliance's operating frame, which is dominated by Manoj Modi, his right-hand man, and is populated with experienced Indian and expat retail professionals.

Rebuilding vs. Building

For the moment, the spotlight is on Reliance. Ever since Ambani marked out retail as the next business focus area for RIL in 2006, he has been talking about a breakout at almost every shareholder meeting of his flagship. Last year might have been just that. Arvind Singhal, chairman of Technopak Advisors, a retail consultant firm, asks to draw pause and think back. 'Future Group has been in retail for 18 years, Shoppers Stop for 15 years, the Tata group also started 15 years back', he says. 'So, I think, it is remarkable that Reliance has been able to overtake some of them in five to six years'. And now, it has future in its sights. Being a late entrant into the retail business has helped Reliance, feels Abneesh Roy, vice-president of Edelweiss Securities, a financial services and research firm.

'In any new sector, be it airline, telecom or retail, one pioneer gives it a start and it is up to the second player to take it to the next level', he says, pointing out how early pioneers like Shoppers Stop in lifestyle and food retailers in the South are now also-rans. 'Reliance has learnt from the failures of its peers. So, it was able to work out the right permutations and is now in a sweet spot'.

Inside Reliance Retail, the belief is that, as in most global markets, a homegrown retailer will set the marker in India. And Reliance wants to be that homegrown retailer. 'It is like China, where although Walmart and Carrefour have been present for 15–20 years, they are still given a run for their monies by traditional players', says a senior Reliance Retail official, on the condition of anonymity.

Because it has a more significant presence in speciality segments (for example, jewellery or electronics), Reliance is competing not just with the Future Group, but also beyond. 'The market is getting segmented', says Kumar Rajgopalan, president of the Retail Association of India. 'The challenge for Reliance, which is in several formats, including speciality stores such as Reliance Jewels, will be to fight the biggies in such different verticals'.

For instance, Tata's 'Tanishq' is a big competitor in the jewellery space. 'Similarly, in the consumer electronics space, it is pitted against Tata Croma and Vijay Sales, among others'. 'Retailers in consumer electronics have been competing to differentiate themselves with limited success', says the Reliance official. 'We have chosen to do things differently. We are betting big on the services played here, in pre- and after-sales so that it creates a different brand perception and pulls consumers'. Given where the Indian market is now, the position in the pecking order—one or two—is somewhat academic, feels Thomas Varghese, former president of the retail council of the Confederation of Indian industry and current chairman of the CIS National Council of Marketing. 'The organised retail market is still nascent and there is enough room for everyone to grow'.

'We are not looking at taking a pie of the existing market and are focused on growing the market', says the Reliance official. Several Future

Group officials, who spoke off the record for this story, expressed a similar line of thought.

The Future Group, anyway, has plenty to think about besides growth. Years of unfettered growth, fuelled by debt, caught up with it. 'Earlier, there was nothing to lose. So, there was less fear during the stage of creation. Today, there is another fear, of losing what we created', he told ET last month. Most of 2012 was about course correction. It saw Biyani sell some businesses completely (financial services and insurance) and give up significant ownership in others (Pantaloons). And it saw Biyani return from driving from the back seat to taking the steering wheel again.

Intuition vs. Precision

Biyani is back roaming the stores, trying to figure out the Indian consumer and crack the retail code. In the way he built Future Group, Biyani relied immensely on intuition and on-the-ground observations. A senior Future Group official, who did not want to be named, narrates one such incident. 'We were standing in front of one of our stores. KB (as everyone calls him) predicted what the sales would be at the end of the day within an hour of observing consumers coming out with various sizes of bags', he says. 'He did not need a calculated system projecting target sales'.

Ambani does walk the Reliance aisles, and even passes on feedback down the rank and file. But his frequency and intensity are nothing compared to that of Biyani, who goes into the granular during his regular store visits and is not even averse to making it company policy. 'He would observe consumers from different income strata or communities and comment on how a particular community had begun shopping at their stores or how a particular community was conspicuous by their absence'. If the focus of the Future Group has been the front end, Reliance's has been the back end, the less visible and the less glamorous part of the retail business.

'The effort begins before the match', says the Reliance official. Reliance approached the supply chain and processes with its trademark engineering mindset and with help from retail professionals who cut their teeth in the world's biggest and best retailers. Its two big hires came in 2011: Rob Cissell, former chief operating officer of Walmart China, was drafted in as CEO of Reliance Value Retail; and Shawn Gray, who headed store operations in the Chinese company, came in as COO. 'The supply chain cannot be outsourced, it is the heart of the business', Cissell told ET in August 2012.

Singhal of Technopak says this sharp focus on the backend has been critical to Reliance's relative success. 'Reliance built a strong foundation for the business not just in terms of IT, but also in terms of hiring the right kind of talent and consultants from all across the world with the right knowledge', he says. 'So, they did not have to make all the mistakes themselves. That industrial mindset to focus on logistics, distribution and supply chain helped'.

The Reliance official cites Reliance Trends, its fashion format, as an example of an efficient back end creating value at the frontend. 'The entire business was engineered in a way that sourcing capability, designers, supply chain and distribution were in the right sync to ensure that affordable, yet fashionable, products reached the consumer in the right fashion cycle', he says. Acknowledging the strides Reliance has taken in many facets of the retail business, Singhal feels the company is still weak on the soft skills needed in a consumer-facing business. 'To proactively anticipate customer needs, which is partly science, intuition and emotions', he says. 'India has been an under-served market. So, consumers have been very generous with system flaws initially. But they are getting more aspirational and Reliance will have to shift gears and lay more emphasis on consumer-facing attributes'.

Family vs. Professionals

The wheels of change in Reliance are being driven by a battery of professionals, including about 10 expats and several old Future group hands. 'It used expats and experts with different skills from various global retail entities with a consistency that Future Group did not', says Roy. 'One is very entrepreneur-led and the other has a very corporate approach', adds Varghese. About two years back, Biyani had moved out of day-to-day operations in the Future Group, and the organization was seen as having lost some of its energy. He's back now, and stamping his presence. 'I am bringing in fresh energy into the business. Employees look towards their leader for inspiration and I realise that I have to do that', he told ET last month.

Reliance Retail, by comparison, is led by Manoj Modi, Mukesh's loyal lieutenant. For all of Reliance being a promoter-led operation and Modi's influence, Reliance Retail is seen as a collective where a vision has been communicated and the second and third rungs are empowered. 'In Reliance Retail, there are no tall people', says the Reliance official. 'We are like an army'. This official adds that select individuals cannot make a difference in the retail business. 'Our culture is built with a focus on the supply chain and is very process-oriented', he says. 'We are paranoid about processes. It is a religion for us. So, at times, it may seem bureaucratic'.

While the contrasts will shape their choices and outcomes, both outfits can stand tall in their respective territories without bothering about competing with each other, feels Kavil Ramachandran, professor at the Indian School of Business. 'At the end of the day, RoI (return on investment) is more important than mere generation of turnover', he says. 'And as an entrepreneur, probably, Biyani has more flexibility to move faster than a large corporate like Reliance. Having said that, nothing would stop Reliance in its growth path given its background of setting an ambitious vision and backing it with adequate resources and a "do it" culture'.

Conclusions

It is necessary to merge with companies to attract investors and growth of the company. Merging helps to create a good vision and mission for the company. Companies are usually in their initial phase of growth and their stocks have the potential for substantial appreciation in price. There are several key factors that must be considered when evaluating investment of growth.

Case Questions

1. How would you analyse the two distinct business management strategies applied by the Biyanis of the Future Group and the giants Ambanis? Which one do you think will be a winner in the long run?

2. With the relaxed FDI norms (in spite of certain regulatory hurdles) and the influx of global retail giants in the Indian retail scenario. There obviously is likely to be a tough fight between entrepreneurial approach (followed by many existing Indian retail companies) and highly professionalized and time-tested global giants warring for space in the highly promising organized retail segment in India. How would you rate the prospects for the existing players in the long term.?

3. What is important in the likely future scenario-focus on frontend retail or effective management of the logistics of retail (backend) in terms of product quality and customer?

20

The First Mover Disadvantage

Learning Objectives

In marketing products of personal health and hygiene, customer perception of value for money and superior in performance and status trend-setter are few of the aspects as very important to make an impact on first-time products to first time users.

As first mover, the company has taken adequate care that its marketing USPs are kept as unique and protected from quick copying by competition who also would like to exploit your product defects as main things which their products have taken care of which helps them to put a peg as a roadblock for the first mover.

The students of marketing management will find this case study as interesting in learning about ways in which a first mover can sustain market and market leadership.

Synopsis

Fresh Feel had pioneered wet wipes in India but could not grow the market. Now new competitors are more successful than the pioneer. What should Fresh Feel do to regain its first mover advantage?

Advaith Hariharan, Manager Fresh Feel Company wondered just what his company's strategy should be. Fresh had spotted the opportunity in 'wet wipes' way back in March 1987, but had failed to educate the consumer about its benefits and convince them to buy the product on a regular basis. 'Had the product been launched ahead of its time in India? Was it because Fresh Feel had just the one product?' wondered Hariharan.

After all, wet wipes was a mature category in Europe and the United States. Leading players such as Ceverly Kern, Gennet & Pern, as well as

Indian Business Case Studies. Srilatha Palekar, Arun Pardhi and Sunanda Jindal, Oxford University Press. © ASM Group of Institutes, Pune, India 2022. DOI: 10.1093/oso/9780192869449.003.0020

smaller firms, had a lineup of brands for different consumer groups and different usage situations.

Case Details

Fresh Feel Personal Care Products Limited was a subsidiary of Zephyr Chemicals & Plastics Limited. The parent company was incorporated on 4 September 1985 as a private limited firm, and went public on 4 March 1986. It made various households and personal care products such as mosquito repellents and wet cleansing tissues under the brand names of 'Japer' and 'Fresh Glow'. In 1990, the company diversified into the manufacturing of polyvinyl chloride (PVC) sheets using technologies acquired from several leading European firms.

This business did so well that within a short time, Zephyr doubled its PVC sheet extrusion line at Silvassa to 4,000 MT per annum. Investments were made in the other businesses also. In the personal care division, modernization was carried out by introducing a new range of household insecticides and the automation of Fresh Glow's production process.

Wet Tissues

Fresh Glow wet tissues came in various ranges and sizes. The ranges were: cologne, lime, baby, intimate, and rose. These were available in packs of 100s, 70s, 50s, 15s, 10s, and 5s. Initially, the wet tissues were packed in plastic containers. The brand name was chosen to connote freshness and used the imagery of water. Hence waves were printed on the pack conveyed the benefit of freshness.

The wet tissues were distributed through super departmental stores, chemists, and general sores. Efforts were made to reach out to the target consumers. The company demonstrated the product at lifestyle exhibitions to get the consumer to try Fresh Glow.

In the first year of launch, sales touched Rs 6,940,000 but dipped the next year badly to Rs 3,000,000. Some modifications in the packaging and the launch of sachet packs revived flagging sales which climbed to Rs 4,940,000 in year three. However, the consumer still did not fancy the product and sales slowly declined to Rs 2,990,000 in FY91 and to a dismal Rs 1,990,000 in FY92.

The Indian Market

Fresh Glow's performance has to be seen in the light of the sector's performance in general. The Rs 6 billion Indian paper tissue market itself was not organized, let alone the wet tissue market. A few brands such a Spintex and Clearfeel (wet tissues) stood out, while Zenith was a smaller brand with a national distribution network. Global players such as Ceverly Kern preferred to target hotels, caterers, and hospitals rather than the retail segment. Consumption was low at about 15 gm per person.

Nearly 48 per cent of India's 1 billion people are in the 18–35 age group. Roughly 500 million, residing in both urban and rural areas, could be said to be reasonably aware of international practices and potential users of paper tissues. This section of the population is well educated, receptive to new ideas, and has sufficient disposable income to afford non-woven disposable products.

Stiff Competition

A new entrant, Cessna Industries Limited (CILT), had recently launched its tissues paper business and planned to invest Rs 250 mn over the next five years. Branded 'Flora', its range of products comprised of facial tissues, toilet tissues, serviettes, handkerchiefs, towels, and napkins. CILT planned to correct the dismal market situation and hoped to capture 10 per cent of the market through an organized entry strategy. Flora was initially distributed in Delhi and there were plans to make it available throughout the country within the year. Flora was competitively priced and targeted at both premium and economy segments. The company's investment plans also included finance for brand-building initiatives.

Importing world-class body care products for women and babies for the past two years, Apex International, based in Gurgaon, had become a name to reckon with. The brainchild of Tejas Patel, Apex's range of international products was popular amongst customers. At the peak of the Indian summer, Apex launched an extensive range of facial cleaning products from Clean n Fresh, Turkey. These were soft, gentle, and effective in removing oil or stains from the skin. They were alcohol free and available in a resealable chocolate-sized pack of 20 wipes (handy to be carried in purses) and in an oval-shaped box containing 100 wipes. They also had makeup removal wipes. These alcohol free, pH 5.5 balanced, with vitamin E and extract of Chamomile wipes were available in a pack of twenty thick and soft wipes. A single wipe guaranteed the entire removal of makeup and cleansed the face and moisturized it too.

Clean n Fresh also catered to the need of babies. Their baby wet wipes were available in economy packs of 80, 160, and 240 wipes. Chocolate-sized convenient travel pack of 12 luxury cloth wipes and extra thick wipes in an easy-to-carry pack of 42 were also available.

Apex also imported Pride tissue paper products from Indonesia. Available in six packs of four colours each (perfumed/non-perfumed), Pride was one of the largest ranges of tissue paper handkerchiefs available in India. All products were made from virgin pulp, and hence there were no hazard of rashes. These contained no brightening agents, chemicals, or colouring dyes.

International Trends

Internationally, the various types of wet wipes are available are categorized as baby, facial, hand and body, general purpose, household, floor care, automotive, clean room, surface preparation, printing, primary and emergency health care, long term, and food service. The United States led the way in the use of wet wipes.

According to the Summer Vacation National Cleaning Survey by USA's Soap and Detergent Association (SDA), 44 per cent of the people surveyed bought hand or personal wipes on vacation with them. Meanwhile, 31 per cent considered cleaning/disinfectant wipes a must have vacation item and 14 per cent reported the use of stain wipes when traveling.

According to market tracker, Euro Monitor, based in Chicago, the global market for disposable consumer-oriented personal care wipes (including adult wipes, baby wipes, and cosmetics wipes such as facial cleansing and deodorant wipes) reached $3.8 billion in 2004. Euro

Monitor expects steady growth to bring the worldwide market to $4.3 billion by 2009. In 2005, the total sale of baby wipes touched $2.5 billion in the global market as compared to $397 million for adult wipes and $886 million for cosmetic wipes.

Meanwhile, in the US market, Information Resources, Inc., a market specialist, estimated baby wipes sales at $404 million and moist towelettes at $580 million from April 2004 to 2005 in the US supermarkets, drug stores, and mass merchandisers. For this period, the top three vendors for baby wipes, according to Information Resources, were Ceverly Kern, Gennet & Parn, and private labels while the top vendors for moist towelettes were Ceverly Kern, Blaypex, and private labels, with Gennet & Parn ranking fourth.

The increasing popularity of specialty wipes for specific applications brought about a decline in baby wipes, which were once used for everything from wiping a baby's bottom to cleaning leather car seats. According to Katharine Rohaz, Category Manager for converting specialist Slimline Industries, baby wipes sales have been flat to slightly trending down due to the introduction of new products. 'Previously consumers used baby wipes for a variety of non-baby purpose. The addition of new products such as household cleaning wipes and feminine hygiene wipes has given consumers products specifically for their needs'.

Susan Everett Stansbury, Right Angle Concepts, Conover, WI, added that not only are application-specific wipes on the rise, multipurpose wipes are also making inroads. 'There are increased options for multipurpose wipes within segments.

From scrubbing to polishing, wipes like these are proliferating everything from skincare to automotive maintenance. So, you can hydrate your skin, cleanse, repair, self-tan, prevent tanning, and so much more that wipes make it easy to do. You can keep your car polished, get special wipes to get bugs off the grill, clean the whitewalls and maintain the leather interior. Wipes materials with various surfaces and characteristics make this possible, along with numerous additives'.

Indeed, wipes of all types are finding new application possibilities and making the most of packaging and scent innovations as well. The introduction of Gennet & Pern's Campers Fundoo and the recent restage of Only Children from Ceverly Kern brought innovative packaging to the toddler wipe market. Scent innovation and special ingredients were also active areas, leading to line extensions in the baby wipe and facial cleanser markets.

In the baby and toddler care category, Gennet & Parn's 2004 Fundoo introduction represents an innovative product line for toddlers that include foaming hand soap and flushable wipes for use during potty training. Fundoo products are designed for toddlers: the foaming hand soap had a larger depressor designed for little hands and fingers and the wipes were kid-sized and came in an easy-to-use, pop-up tub.

For its part, consumer product giant Ceverly Ken is also leveraged the strength of its top baby brand to launch several new products in the kid care category. Two such innovations were the new disposable Nappies Washcloths and Nappies Wash Mitts, which were made from a proprietary, multilayered, composite material manufactured to provide optimal strength, flexibility, thickness, softness, and texture.

The combination of these properties provided gentle cleaning with cloth-like durability. To further enhance product performance, a secondary process impregnates the wipe with a lathering baby wash solution capable of lasting throughout the bathing experience.

Recce-Pak was another company taking advantage of opportunities to compete in the private label kids wipes area. Racce-Pak had several new personal care products, including Cool Wipes, which was scheduled to hit the stores in the fall. The wipes were positioned to provide a value price brand for the growing toddler pre-moistened toilet wipes market. Racce-Pak offered 50 wipes in a brightly coloured press-top tub and a 50 count resealable refill.

In the facial cleansing area, some wet wipe products were moving beyond basic cleansing and offering additional consumer benefits and treatments, such as anti-ageing, anti-acne, exfoliating, and sensitive skin facial wipes. Demographic and lifestyle changes expected to influence the development of new moist wipes products in this segment include the ageing of the population, the increase of 'metro-sexual' men who are more appearance conscious and the wider distribution of premium-priced products as the line between mass and class blurs.

'Consumer desire for convenience and cleanliness will continue to drive the personal care wipe market', Rece-Pak's Connor said. 'We know that facial wipes are viewed as a convenient alternative to other facial cleansing products. And in our time-pressed society, the desire for convenience is only going to increase. Likewise, moist toilet tissue is a convenient, hygienic tool for mothers who are toilet training toddlers'.

While key players such as Ceverly Kenn ere phasing out facial cleansing cloths, plenty of other producers were lining up to fill any gaps on store shelves. G & P's Floay daily facials wipes delivered cleansing and care in one step while Mill's offered cleansing towelettes for a variety of applications.

The company also launched Mill's Exfoliating Cleansing towelettes, a pre-moistened wipe with cucumber extract for everyday exfoliation. The towelettes are formulated with microbeads to renew and refresh skin with every use.

Last year, Floay launched its own wet cloth for facial cleaning and caring. Floay Daily Facial Express is a 10-second facial treatment designed to lock dirt into the cloth and lift it away from the skin, leaving the skin soft and clean.

Looking forward, further trends include consumer-appealing packaging, new fragrances, different wet wipe lotions, and even more products designed to meet specific needs (such as feminine hygiene wipes). Portable wet wipes for cars, purses, backpacks, and lunch boxes are predicted to benefit from an increasingly germ-conscious society.

In terms of technologies, many companies were keeping a sharp eye on the growth of spun lace use for wipes products, particularly baby wipes. Flushability and biodegradability were expected to remain key issues as the personal care wipes industry moved forward. In fact, Association of the Nonwoven Fabrics Industry (INDA) and (the European Disposable and Nonwovens Association (EDANA) have established a joint task force examining standards for determining flushability.

Fresh Feel's Dilemma

Hariharan convened a meeting of his core team and discussed the market scenario. He said, 'The strong Indian middle class of 250mn has purchasing power and living standards nearly equivalent to the middle class of developed countries. They tend to use the products based on availability and convenience. The children in these families are potential customers for all kinds of baby diapers and baby wipes'.

'Further as a concept, wet wipes in the beginning can catch up only in restaurants and in travel situations'. Carded chemical bonded and spun bond polypropylene is the most common wet wipe used in the country by airlines and other establishments. On the supermarket shelves, some local converters offer the wet wipes made from spunlace nonwovens, explained Reena Gupta, strategy consultant. Sanner Dayte, Senior VP, South Zone, chipped in, 'The current low penetration of these products has provided a fertile market for new entrants to India.

However, Indian customers are value driven, hence only a product with a true value will succeed. The high birth rate also ensures a recurring huge demand for infant-related nonwoven products. Baby wipes is expected to grow rapidly among the urban population, whereas the general moistened wipes will take some more time for the concept to be accepted by the Indian population' (Sunday Times Weekly News Supplement with TOI).

Case Questions

1. How would you explain the failure of Fresh Feel in not capitalizing on their maiden product line, the wet wipes, which when imitated as towelettes and wipe sheets by other manufacturers, were preferred at the markets? Why could Fresh Feel not as a first mover in the market hasten up product modification of wet wipes and appear diffident when faced by competitor products?

2. It confirms the learned view that products meant for personal use, such wet wipes and baby wipes are extremely value-sensitive products and if there is no USP element in the product, soon one is likely to be thrown out of the market created by them as first movers by competitions which picks up feedback from Fresh Feel customers and introduces products by implementing a new USP which offers better value than Fresh Feel. Is it not surprising that First Feel did not use the business secrecy and intellectual rights clauses to sustain competitive advantage and sustainable product line?

Milton Keynes UK
Ingram Content Group UK Ltd.
UKHW020228211223
434768UK00002B/9